BOARDING PASSES
TO FARAWAY PLACES

by Guy A. Sibilla

with aloha

6 November 2019

ARCHWAY
PUBLISHING

Archway Publishing books may be ordered through booksellers or by contacting:

Archway Publishing
1663 Liberty Drive
Bloomington, IN 47403
www.archwaypublishing.com
1 (888) 242-5904

Because of the dynamic nature of the Internet, any web addresses or
links contained in this book may have changed since publication and
may no longer be valid. The views expressed in this work are solely those
of the author and do not necessarily reflect the views of the publisher,
and the publisher hereby disclaims any responsibility for them.

ISBN: 978-1-4808-4691-3 (clothbound)
ISBN: 978-1-4808-4692-0 (perfect bound)
ISBN: 978-1-4808-4693-7 (electronic)

Library of Congress Control Number: 2017910367

Printed in the United States if America.

Archway Publishing rev. date: 9/13/2017

To my father, Anthony John Sibilla, in memoriam,
and to my mother, Evelyn Murashige Sibilla,
for having such a love of the world.

Her husband's to Aleppo gone, master o' the Tiger

—William Shakespeare, *MacBeth*
(Act 1, Scene 3; c. 1606)

BOARDING PASSES
TO FARAWAY PLACES

CONTENTS

INTRODUCTION

By the time I had entered my teens, I had already spent half of my life abroad.

People travel for all kinds of reasons. Some take vacations to connect with their past, to satisfy their intellectual curiosity by visiting historical sites, to enjoy foreign food and wine, or simply to get away from humdrum daily life. I lump all of this activity together as tourism in one form or another, which involves round-trip journeys with the details of a trip being planned before departure. When people who travel in this fashion arrive back home, they simply pick up where they had left off.

When my family packed for a trip, we weren't going on holiday. Unlike vacation travelers, we moved in only one direction. My father was a chief warrant officer (CW3) in the United States Army as a computer systems analyst. CWO Sibilla's orders to transfer to another post, whether abroad or stateside, were also our orders in that we were moving away.

When Dad's orders arrived, I said goodbye to friends and family. I withdrew from school. My parents sold our house. Bank accounts were closed. Mail was forwarded to my uncle Lee's home in Pennsylvania. Our neighbors who grew up and stayed in the same place all their lives must have been dismayed to discover one day that we were gone. Forever.

Travel wasn't a break from life; it *was* our life.

I was the son of a Japanese mother from Honolulu and an Italian father from Philadelphia. As cliché as it may sound, they met on Waikīkī Beach. They were fiercely devoted to one another for fifty-two years, until the day he died. He served his country with distinction for twenty-five years of his adult life, during which time the army regularly moved us around.

As I grew into my own life, I began to understand that the very concept of travel almost prevented me from being born. In unraveling some of the mysteries of my own family history, I learned that my Japanese grandparents didn't support my father's and mother's desire to marry. As handsome as he was to my mother, my father was Italian, which made him *gaijin*. He was a Roman Catholic who had walked into a Buddhist home. But most disagreeably, he was in the United States Army, which meant that my Japanese grandparents feared he would take my mother, Akiko, away from them.

In 1950, they got married anyway, and in short order, my father did just as my mother's parents feared. I imagine my mother sitting on the wooden floor of my grandparents' home in Palōlō Valley as she told Grandma Naoye that we were "moving overseas" to a place called Germany. Her father, Kumeo, and her mother must have wept privately at the news. Travel was taking their daughter away.

In this way, the idea of travel entered my psyche as one-way movement. As the journey to proceed to a place "outside of the country" began, the approaching unknown evoked a sense of excitement. Newness awaited us across two seas and a continent. And at five years old, I already understood that each day was another step forward in our journey of discovery.

My mother explained what was happening in simple terms. My two sisters and I were told we were going far from the beaches we knew, so far away, in fact, that we needed to wear shoes and buy winter coats. We moved by airplane, by car, by train, and by boat. At each transit area, I focused my eyes on the oddities around me. Each distant city reaffirmed that we had arrived onto a strange, new, fascinating planet.

It would be decades later before I realized that my parents had led me down a path I would follow for the remainder of my life. They laughed, held hands, and made my sisters and I feel safe in the face of the dizzying pace of changing scenery, customs, food, clothing, people, odors, and language. My parents were fearless. And if they had nothing to fear, then neither did I.

Travel filled each day with wonder. I thought that everyone had grown up speaking another language. I assumed it was normal to translate the cost of bread for my mother at the market so my mom could pay in deutsche marks. I believed all Boy Scouts got to camp in Switzerland with other scouts from France, Spain, Germany, and Belgium. I supposed it was normal to pass military police with your ID in hand each time you went through the gate to get onto base. I thought everyone explored medieval castles on weekends. Food, money, music, history, architecture, colors, art, fabric, graphic design, plants, trees, cars, buses, and every other detail of life changed every time we moved.

We wove into the rhythm of our lives an expectation of flux every few years. As birthdays accrued and the second winter came and went, we knew we would be traveling soon. That meant we would again be adapting to new food and clothing and customs and schools—maybe a new language. We adjusted quickly. With every move, we revised ourselves.

Entering a new school every few years wasn't as difficult as it sounds. At times, though, we realized we lived differently than most people. I recalled for my new classmates our eating *wienerwurst* at the *marktplatz* in Würzburg and our time in Heidelberg with our German babysitter, Gelinda. School friends envied my tales of our one-way, nine-and-a-half-hour turboprop airliner adventures from Honolulu to San Francisco. Back then, that was fast and we were jet-setters, even though the engines had propellers.

My family had driven across the United States four times and passed through thirty states. We once took a military transport ship, the USS *Wm. O. Darby*, from New York to Bremerhaven. While crossing the North Atlantic Ocean, we got caught in a storm so severe that we had to practice "abandon ship" drills.

I had hiked, camped, and climbed mountains in Switzerland with the Boy Scouts. When we were in Chicago, my father took me to the old Comiskey Park to see the White Sox play. I had eaten beignets in New Orleans, hoagies in Philadelphia, bratwurst in Wiesbaden, and raw fish in Hawaii.

Life was amazing.

I got used to introducing myself and to explaining where I had just come from and where my family had been before that. Maybe that's how I learned of the delight in telling stories.

This roaming lifestyle was wonderful preparation for college. After two years of study at George Mason University in the Washington, DC, suburbs, I transferred to the College of William and Mary in Williamsburg, Virginia. Three years later, I confronted an ill-defined destiny. I sat quietly in my academic counselor's office as she reviewed my transcript and, upon doing so, asked me quite bluntly, "For exactly what are you preparing yourself to do?"

I had no response. I had dabbled in the entire palette of educational colors listed in the course book. My course load appeared so random that it looked like I had thrown darts at the class listings to choose my schedule. I took classes in anthropology, US history, English literature, music, European history, government, art history, German, American literature, Italian, English poetry, archery, introduction to law, sociology, orienteering, and so on. I attended lectures on ethics, astronomy, music composition, Mesoamerican pottery, Greek and Roman sculptors, the politics of the Middle East, the politics of Europe, the politics of the South America, the politics of Southeast Asia, psychology, journalism, photography, engineering, and so forth. I couldn't read enough books, hear enough music, see enough plays, listen to enough lectures, or watch enough movies. Enough was never enough when it came to the world of ideas, because those ideas gave context to the world I had already drifted across.

I didn't know it then, but over thirty years later I finally had an answer. I had been preparing myself to be a travel writer. I have now spent my life in large part moving across the earth and writing about it for magazines, newspapers, and just about any media outlet that had an audience who liked stories from distant exotic places. One time I received an award at a banquet held by the Hawaii Chapter of the Society of Professional Journalists, but I was away at the time. I preferred to spend my money on travel.

I didn't need a lot of money because I avoided tourist destinations with their expensive hotels and buffets. Instead, I set out on foot, on trains, on buses, in canoes, and occasionally on horseback. I slept on the ground in deserts and in tents in jungles. I carried my clothing, a journal, a camera, and a medical kit in a small backpack. Wherever I ended up, even for a day, I was home.

When I wasn't on the road, I was planning my next outing and worked with a law firm to gather funds. In college I took my degree in government and English literature and then, on a whim, went to law school.

I have always been a serious student, but the endless hours of reading legalese was mind-numbing. In response, I fell back on the literature I knew and cherished. As a first-year law student, on occasion I would write my case synopses in rhyme. Sometimes I wrote jokingly of the silly disputes, knowing I would never be called upon to read one of those synopses in class.

I was wrong. But to this day my classmates still discuss with glee my rendition of a contracts case. That was, by the way, the first and last time my contracts professor ever called on me to recite a case. He found it impossible to apply the Socratic method while laughing.

Much to the dismay of my parents and a few friends, I abandoned the security of a law career for a considerably less secure one as a travel writer. I explained, "Law just didn't sing to me." I confess I don't know what that means, even though I made that reason up myself. I do know, however, that even after all of these years, travel writing still sings to me, and continues to do so every day.

Fair warning: the following pages will not serve you well (if at all) as a travel guidebook. Instead, this is a work of literary nonfiction that recounts my oftentimes not-so-well-thought-through travel escapades. So if you understand that curiosity peppered with a healthy dose of wanderlust is a force so powerful that it can cause you to forsake your house, your car, secure employment, health insurance, and stable relationships, then these stories are for you.

One of my dearest friends and longtime editor in chief of *Honolulu Magazine*, Mr. John Heckathorn, described my exploits as "adventure travel" journalism. Although he would never want to do what I did, he relished the drama of my drifting around for months at a time gathering stories. Upon my return from the Middle East, he announced in his column in the *Honolulu Star-Bulletin*, "Sibilla Survives Syria!"

On another occasion, I told him I was headed to Pakistan to cover the fiftieth anniversary of the first ascent of K2 by the Italians. He commented with concern, "You realize, of course, that you're flying into a city whose name has *Islam* and *bad* in it?" He was joking, but he only did so to hide his worry.

"You can't let fear stop you!" I offered with optimism to calm his concerns while masking my own anxieties.

Newspaper accounts or magazine pieces are often about destinations. *Boarding Passes to Faraway Places* contains travelogues chiefly about the act of movement itself. It is about the diversity of the people across our planet and their kindness when faced with my ever-amusing state of perpetual confusion and disorientation.

This collection begins with the most exotic, disgusting, enchanting, appalling, poetic, filthy, bewildering, beguiling place on earth: India. If you have been there, you'll feel me on this. If you haven't, grab a whiskey or a cup of Darjeeling, plop into a soft chair, and enjoy the ride—without the diarrhea. Two other stories set on the subcontinent unfold from countries identified on the US State Department's "Warnings and Alerts" list, Myanmar (aka Burma) and Pakistan.

One of my favorite stories takes place in the Middle East when I traversed Syria and Jordan in 2007 just before the Arab Spring. I was ceaselessly enchanted by the ancient cities of Damascus, Aleppo, and Palmyra. I spent blissful evenings eating sweets, drinking Turkish coffee, and witnessing life at the street level as it has been for thousands of years.

The Syrians and Jordanians were gracious, generous, quick to smile, and always helpful. I hold onto these joyful memories in the face of the heartbreaking televised news that I see almost daily displaying the incomprehensible human tragedy and senseless destruction of this glorious region of our world.

There is a story of Africa wherein I recount how Chief Guendon in Lomé, Togo, helped me get my mojo on. Voodoo isn't as scary as you may think.

One of my more lighthearted narratives takes place in Central America. While traipsing through the jungles of Belize, Guatemala, and Mexico with a team of anthropologists, I stumbled upon a previously undiscovered Maya village, which now bears the name "Guy's Group" on some map somewhere in the School of Anthropology at the University of Texas–San Antonio.

I conclude with two stories from my neighborhood in the Pacific Ocean. One time, I slept with the *moai* on Rapa Nui (aka Easter Island), and on another occasion, I entered a war zone in Timor-Leste (aka East Timor) to cover a story on the United Nations Peacekeeping Forces from Fiji.

This was not one continuous journey around the world. Rather, *Boarding Passes to Faraway Places* recounts some of my travels taken at various times from 2000 through 2007. I believe it was A. A. Gill, one of the world's great contemporary writers, who suggested that you really don't grasp fully the impact a journey has had on you until you have returned home and have let the memories steep for a while. I agree. These excursions finally make enough sense for me to write about them.

Even after the passage of time, or perhaps because of it, I am especially amused recalling how the suggestions of strangers so easily influenced me to take a train, a plane, a boat, or a car in a direction

I had not otherwise planned. I was constantly amazed at where I ended up and at the people I met along the way.

That sense of wonderment comes from wandering, from arriving without a plan, and from the feeling of exuberance you experience when you let go and allow the path to choose you.

SINCE YOU LAST DEPARTED
THE IMPERIAL

It was Friday the thirteenth in India.

I was in Delhi in September of 2000 and it was so excruciatingly hot that not only were the armpits of my shirt soaking wet but also patches of perspiration showed through my khaki pants behind my knees. I didn't even know the human body could sweat there. I can assure you, though, that when you have knee-pit sweat, you either are standing fully clothed in a sauna or are in India in the summer.

I wasn't there on assignment, but I had been to India before. The one item on my agenda was to visit my friend Tenzin Kalsang B, a Tibetan monk who lived in Namgyal Monastery with the Dalai Lama. In an effort to beat back jet lag, I was wandering around Delhi to get oriented to the city, find the train station, and check out the Chandni Chowk, the old marketplace.

I did manage to find the Special Foreign Booking Office on the second floor of the New Delhi Railway Station and make my travel arrangements. The monsoon rains had flooded the roads in and around Delhi. I knew, though, that I could count on the Indian Railway System.

That evening, my northbound train was speeding through Himachal Pradesh. I was headed toward Pathankot Station near the foothills of the Himalayas, having departed New Delhi at 9:00 p.m., sort of, to arrive the following morning at 8:00 a.m. From Pathankot Station, I planned to hire a car and driver to take me to McLeod Ganj, a town adjacent to Dharamsala, the seat of the Tibetan government-in-exile.

Tenzin Kalsang B lived at the end of the clouds in Namgyal Monastery about fifty-eight hundred feet above the Punjabi plains. Our friendship had begun several years earlier, far from the cool, lofty mountains of Dharamsala. We met, instead, on the sweltering plains of Uttar Pradesh at a tiny Tibetan temple in Kushinagar.

Kushinagar in eastern Uttar Pradesh is as remote as it is small. It is not a tourist destination. It has no airport. It does not even have a train station, which is saying something in a country that boasts one of the world's most extensive railway systems.

At other times in its history, Kushinagar had been known as Kushawati or Kushinara. Regardless of its name, it has been the end point for Buddhist pilgrims since the fifth century BCE. The remnants of Buddha's cremation stupa mark the location of his last breath. This is the only reason that Kushinagar exists at all.

As destiny is known to do, Tenzin Kalsang B and I became friends on account of random chance. A single sentence buried in over one thousand pages of my guidebook suggested that for a modest donation, I could stay overnight in a Tibetan monastery in Kushinagar. Thus, before I had even landed in India, I knew I was going to try my hand at living on monk time.

To get to Kushinagar, I had to fly to Varanasi and then hire a car and driver. While making arrangements, I booked myself a few days' stay at the Imperial Hotel on Janpath. Since then, with nearly a decade of travel across India, the luxuriant Imperial Hotel has become the beginning and ending point of every journey I have ever taken on the subcontinent.

The word *lavish* does not quite capture the atmosphere of this carved-mahogany, marble-floored, canopied-four-poster-bed, Victorian-style oasis. It is like living in a museum dedicated to re-creating the period at the apex of the British Empire. To give you a sense of how old school this colonial-style hotel is, it had the cable address COMFORT. The most recent use of the word *cable* I could find in an actual conversation was in a period movie set in the forties when messages were sent via telegraph lines.

Further evidence of Great Britain's colonial influence was reflected in the envelope holding my room key, which instructed the following:

FOREIGNERS SHOULD PAY

THEIR BILLS IN ACCEPTABLE

FOREIGN CURRENCY

That sounded a lot like something I might have read in the classic travelogue *A Goddess in the Stones* by Norman Lewis. I wasn't entirely sure how that admonition affected me directly, since the cashier at the hotel took my American Express card.

I secretly coveted the idea that the hotel maintained a minimum, albeit undisclosed, standard of what they considered to be "acceptable foreign currency." I may be going out on a limb here, but I bet the cashier wouldn't have accepted my kwacha from Zambia. Or my kina from Papua New Guinea. Or my quetzals from Guatemala. Even the word *foreign* sounded foreign here.

What also felt a little odd was the personal housekeeper posted outside my room. His employment required that he wait at my beck and call, apparently twenty-four hours a day.

I started out feeling like I was being pampered. Later it felt just the opposite. Sometime around midnight, I left my room because jet lag told my brain it was morning in my time zone. When I flung open my door, I was startled to see Vikram. He scared the crap out of me. Maybe I did the same, as he jumped up from his chair perched next to my doorway.

Vikram stood erect as if I were his drill sergeant and he was being reviewed for inspection. He wore a black shirt that draped over his bony shoulders, with matching pants and slippers. He smiled much too brightly for me at that time in the morning.

"Mr. Guy! Good day! What may I do for you, sir?" he asked

politely. The marble-floored hallway stretched in both directions as silent as a morgue. It was so quiet you would never suspect there were over a billion Indians waiting beyond the Imperial's walled courtyard.

"Namaste!" I think I grunted. Then I smiled and waved at him as I headed out of the hotel. Anyone who knows me knows that I am barely attached to this planet before I have a cup of coffee. This encounter is emblematic, though, of how far the Imperial Hotel goes to provide Old World service in a New World era.

Later that morning I met with Amit, assistant front office desk manager, for whom no request was too small or too difficult in helping with travel plans to Kushinagar. He was tall, outfitted in a marvelously tailored black suit and starched white shirt, and had slicked-back black hair. He spoke deliberately, like a school head-master, minus the condescension. Instead he seemed thrilled I was anxious to explore his expansive country.

With not so much as a blink, the Imperial Hotel service ma-chinery kicked into gear. Amit arranged an encashment certificate with the hotel cashier, which allowed me to exchange United States dollars for Indian rupees. That was my first experience face-to-face with India's legendary caste system.

The assistant to the assistant cashier was a very pretty Indian woman who stood no farther than ten feet away from Amit. Rather than carry the encashment certificate to her, Amit called her on the phone. I could hear both of them clearly as they spoke to one another. I looked at Amit as he asked her to retrieve the document for her review. I then looked over at her and listened as she agreed to do so.

I watched her take a dozen steps or so across the lobby to where we were seated and then carry the document back to her desk. She banged it with a red-ink stamp and then delivered it to someone standing next to her who appeared to be a person who may have had access to the desired Indian rupees.

This gentleman took the encashment certificate and went

someplace else, returning sometime later with bills. The entire process for transferring the rupees to me was the same as I had witnessed previously, except in reverse. I am a patient man, but even I gaped at the Kabuki theater on display following my simple request to exchange funds.

This entire affair brought me back to something Salman Rushdie, who wrote the unforgettable *Midnight's Children*, observed. When commenting on India and the Hindi language, he notably remarked, "No people whose word for 'yesterday' is the same as their word for 'tomorrow' can be said to have a firm grip on [the concept of] time." At that moment, while sitting quietly at Amit's desk, I understood exactly what Salman meant.

I excused myself and left the details for airline tickets to Varanasi to Amit's good office. Shortly thereafter I was told I was set to depart for Lal Bahadur Shastri Airport in a few days' time.

When the time came, I appeared at the Indian Airlines check-in counter at the Delhi airport. Oddly, I was issued my boarding pass on the morning of my departure and was assigned seat 11F. However, when I passed through security, my first boarding pass was taken from me and I was given another boarding pass, this one indicating my seat was now "Any." Like the protocol for changing money at the Imperial, this was just one of many things in India that occurred for which there was no ready explanation.

In Varanasi, fate took charge, as it always did. I slung my pack containing all of my belongings. As I left the baggage area, I was mobbed by a slew of shouting touts.

The afternoon heat did not seem to affect the army of small children with their dark hair, big eyes, and outstretched hands. Some wore tattered, colorless cotton clothing. I glimpsed bare feet. There were boys and girls who looked like they were eight to ten years old, but in the flurry of words and furtive movement, it was impossible to tell which was which.

In the desperate competition for compensation, hands pulled on my shirtsleeves. I felt other hands yank on my belt. Someone tugged on my backpack. The only way these children made money was to get me to go to their waiting driver—and there was no way for me to tell who was working for whom in the middle of this lot filled with parked cars and men standing next to them watching me watching them.

"Hello, mister!"

"Where are you from?"

"Where are you going?"

"You need ride?"

Out of this chaos, I secured a ride, the tout got paid his baksheesh, and the driver made some money for his family. We all got what we wanted, and no one got hurt. This scenario replayed itself countless times at every transit area in India, whether I traveled by airplane, bus, or train.

That's how I met Arif Khan. His tout dragged me by my hand and delivered me to his car. Arif's name card read as follows:

Arif Khan, Driver
Authorised to Carry all Visiting tourist [sic]
Car No. UP 32 A 2758

I liked his smile, and he wasn't pushy like the kid who had pushed me toward him. I gave his tout some rupees, and the child ran off looking for more tourist bait.

"Arif Khan?" I asked upon reading his card. "As-salaam alaikum!" I said, placing my hand over my heart, expressing my hope that the blessings of God be upon him. I surmised he was Muslim by his name.

"Wa alaikum salaam!" he replied, smiling (May the blessings of God be upon you too). "I am pleased we meet, sir! Where are you staying?"

"Don't know," I confessed, knowing he would suggest someplace. "Any ideas?" I asked.

"Sir, please allow me! I know a place with my friend. It is very,

very nice, sir. It is called Hotel Clarks Varanasi. You will like this place very much, sir!" With that, off we sped toward Arif's baksheesh and my room.

After a short ride, I got out of the car and was introduced to Nitin, whom I suspected was Arif's cousin, brother-in-law, actual brother, or business partner. Regardless, he was quite nice and well-spoken. The deal was done.

The Hotel Clarks was comfortable by most standards. It was quiet, clean, and away from the din of worshippers who inundated the banks of the Ganges daily. I settled in and decided to wander around Varanasi for a few days to see if I could get my third eye focused. I'm not a Hindu, mind you. In fact, Hinduism is not a proselytizing religion; you can't be converted to it. You are simply born Hindu or you are not.

Still, I like the spiritual nature of Hinduism and the idea that my third eye represents the gateway to the inner realms of higher consciousness. I think it is self-evident that, as human beings, we are all seekers of enlightenment. I aspired to do well or, at a minimum, do no harm. Avoiding bad karma was one way of trying to ensure happiness in my next life.

Unlike me, Hindu pilgrims bathe in the Ganges River to wash away their sins. Given that the Ganges is famous for its cremations, Hindus believe that being cremated here breaks the cycle of death and rebirth and ushers the dead directly to heaven. It is more than a place at the confluence of the Varuna and Asi Rivers. Varanasi is the center of the Hindu world.

In Europe, many of the old towns and villages have an ancient charm to them, a kind of patina of majesty brought on with age. In Varanasi, age has a different effect. The landscape is filled with an array of dilapidated, disfigured, and crumbling structures made to appear even more fragile by their muted colors. This is not a repugnant sight. In fact, Varanasi has a peculiarly luminous quality to it.

A salmon-colored ghat (a building with steps leading to the Ganges) adjoined the pale yellow façade of a structure with bamboo green trim. There were so many scars on the face of an old Rajasthani sandstone ghat that it had the feel of Monet's *Rouen Cathedral*. It seemed more illusion than real. All along the shoreline were the tones of tangerine, mustard, onionskin, yellow squash, and Anjou pears.

The air filled with the scent of cooking oil as roti (unleavened bread) was fried on flat metal griddles in food stalls lining the streets. I winced as I walked through narrow passageways with suffocating head-high walls lined with cow-dung patties pressed against the wall to dry, to be used later as fuel. I kept zigzagging my way toward the river, offering a smile and an occasional "Namaste!" to those who appeared Hindu.

Funeral pyres filled the air with smoke as fire cleansed bodies of the dead enfolded in white shrouds on their final transformation back to nature's five essential elements: earth, sky, air, fire, and of course, water. Mother Ganges would be home to their ashes once the fire had done its work.

After a few days of exploring wondrous Varanasi, I needed to hire a car and driver to take me to what had brought me here in the first place: Kushinagar. I asked Arif for his help. Within a day, he quoted me a price to rent a Hindustan Ambassador, pay a driver, and buy petrol.

I was introduced to Arun, a lanky, slightly older-appearing man with glazed-over eyes and teeth stained permanently red from chewing *paan*. Men in India chew the mixture of betel leaf and areca nut in epidemic proportions. It is said to provide a stimulating psychoactive effect. This effect was not, however, what I thought my driver needed in preparation for our journey of 240 kilometers north along the winding, unlit, unmarked Indian roadways.

I did not know it when we departed from Varanasi that our passage required seven hours of perseverance. We dodged an endless string of huge Tata lorries, smaller trucks, buses, bicyclists, pedestrians, and donkey carts.

I held my breath on more than one occasion as Arun and I

careened around a corner of the narrow country two-lane roads and nearly drove up a looming elephant butthole as an adorned elephant was being featured prominently as part of a wedding parade for a newly married couple. We sped by lush rice paddies pockmarked intermittently by the rusting carcasses of trucks that had run off the roadway. I wondered if those drivers had been chewing paan when their rubber left the road.

We arrived late in the day at the monastery in Kushinagar. I considered kissing the ground as I exited the Ambassador, but I was fearful of the message that would send to Arun. We still had to drive back to Varanasi, once I found the courage to even consider it.

The day was tortuously hot and humid. The temple was not as I had expected. My romanticized, exotically Far Eastern, monastic lifestyle dream came crashing around the stark reality of India. I was not facing a grand house of the holy with its huge, dark halls filled with rows of meditating monks draped in saffron robes quietly shifting their feet.

Functionality had produced a building with the architectural flare of a Quonset hut. Its faded walls, the color of ginger root, had not been able to withstand the effects of poor construction. Flaking, discoloration, and cracks made the structure appear years older than it really was. It was an outpost of grassroots Buddhism.

On that scorching summer afternoon, I wandered through the dilapidated gates and pounded on the front door. A half-robed and not so perky monk stumbled into the sunlight with pillow lines still embossed on the side of his face. I had awakened him from his nap. I took a step back to a safe distance, wondering if Buddhists were allowed to get cranky when aroused from sleep.

"Namaste," I said with an awkward smile. At a slender 5'8," the monk looked boyishly younger than his twenty-one years, if that was possible. I stood across from him with a beseeching look on my face, while he stared back at me as if wondering what in heaven's name I might be doing there in the oppressive heat of the Indian summer.

"Is it okay for me to stay here for a couple of nights?" I asked, although I could sense that this was the wrong time to ask for a favor. I proceeded shamelessly. "And I need a room for my driver too." There was a long pause. I took the monk's silence to mean he was actually considering turning me down.

"Sorry," seemed like a good restart. "I am Guy. I read in my book that if you had room, I could maybe stay here a few nights? With my driver. Is okay?"

Another long pause. This was awkward.

"Okay!" suddenly emerged out of his mouth.

"Nobody here now. You choose room there!" he said, pointing across a scraggly grassed courtyard.

"Shukriya!" I said, placing my hands together, saying thank you. I wished I could've been more polite and expressed myself in a Tibetan dialect instead of Hindi. As I grabbed my gear and walked across the courtyard, I deduced Buddhist lesson no. 1: Do not disturb a monk from his nap.

I set up home in a small cubicle that had a wooden bed, a stool, a tiny table, a candle, and a window. It was austere but welcoming in a cubicle sort of way. The unscreened windows let in the breeze and the sounds of the birds. The flaked paint on the walls softened the hardness of the concrete. And the soft late afternoon light encouraged napping.

When things were somewhat organized, I stretched out under my mosquito net and soon fell asleep under a blanket of warm afternoon breezes. Turnabout, as it is said, is fair play. Later that day, the monk I had disturbed from his afternoon nap came knocking on my door, disturbing me from mine.

When I opened the door, he stood before me holding a small pot of chai in one hand and two glass cups in the other. He introduced himself as Tenzin Kalsang B. Neither of us could have known it then, but from that day forward, our friendship would span over a decade and lead me to visit him a few years later in Dharamsala.

"*Tashi delak!*" he offered in the melodic tones of his Tibetan greeting. "You like chai?" he offered, making it sound more like a statement than a question.

"Yes!" I said, trying to appear awake. "Please, come in." I moved the stool over to the table for him, and then I sat on the edge of the bed. In between sips of a spicy cinnamon tea concocted with buffalo milk, we traded questions about family and friends, our upbringing, and the world at large.

"Most my family live still in Llasa [Tibet]," he began. He hadn't seen them since he'd joined the monastery when he was nine. It was the highest of honors to have a son intelligent enough to endure the rigorous schedule of Buddhist study, which can last fifteen years or more. Whatever sadness their separation may have brought, Tenzin Kalsang B said his family was happy and proud. For hours we shared stories and laughter and ideas.

"Tenzin," I commented innocently, "is a very famous name." I explained that Tenzin Norgay was the Sherpa in Sir Edmund Hillary's autobiography *View from the Summit* who accompanied him on the first conquest of Mt. Everest in 1953.

"Only difference," Tenzin commented, "my name Tenzin Kalsang B."

There was a pause. Curiosity overcame my manners.

"What does the *B* stand for?"

"His Holiness, the Dalai Lama," Tenzin explained, "first name Tenzin. And he give all his name."

I nodded politely.

"My family name Kalsang, so my monk name Tenzin Kalsang." I continued to nod.

"In Namgyal Monastery already monk Tenzin Kalsang. So Dalai Lama say, 'You Tenzin Kalsang A, and I Tenzin Kalsang B.'" Already laughing at his own story, Tenzin Kalsang B didn't need to ask, "It funny, yes?" My laughter was answer enough.

Buddhist lesson no. 2: All solutions do not have to be complicated.

Daily life was simple and began in the open courtyard. We pumped cold water from a well by pushing down on an iron handle and catching the water in buckets. While standing in shorts, we poured the cold water over our heads, lathered soap and shampoo, and rinsed off with another bucket of cold water. I confess, laughing while talking and bathing with others makes daily hygiene fun.

We spent the days strolling about, visiting temples, and walking around stupas (holy structures) telling stories. Afternoons were always spent sharing chai and conversation after a midday nap. For dinner we would walk into town and eat Indian food prepared at a small kitchen.

In the evenings, I spent time in my room making notes in my journal by candlelight. Then with a tiny puff of air from my lips, I was in a dark room with a cool breeze, the sound of cicadas, and peaceful slumber.

The days lolled by one after the other at the pace of candle wax dripping. One day, though, it was time to head off. I promised Tenzin Kalsang B that we would meet again in Dharamsala someday in the near future. During the course of our preparations, Tenzin Kalsang B suggested that since Kushinagar was where Buddha died, I should go to Lumbini before returning to Varanasi, because that was where Buddha was born as Siddhārtha Gautama three thousand years ago.

"It close from here!" Tenzin Kalsang B proclaimed. In reality, Lumbini, Nepal, was another 350 kilometers north. Until that moment, I never even knew Lumbini existed.

As G. K. Chesterton famously opined: "A traveller sees what he sees; a tourist sees what he has come to see." Without so much as a second thought, Arun and I sped off again farther northward to see what we could see. I steeled myself beside my paan-stoked, glassy-eyed driver, riding shotgun and keeping my eyes peeled for elephant buttholes.

It all went well. We crossed the border into Nepal and poked around Lumbini for a few days. The days and nights there were even quieter than they were in Kushinagar. If time had moved any slower, it would've stopped altogether.

In contrast, it was an equally exhilarating return drive to

Varanasi. From there I hopped onto a thankfully uneventful Indian Airlines flight back to Delhi. In a state of relief only the hardiest of travelers would understand, I traipsed through the immaculate lobby of the Imperial Hotel in my now dusty and sweaty Varanasi Nepalese-inspired outfit much to the mortification, I am sure, of the other more well-heeled patrons.

The following morning, I rang up Amit, who was delighted to hear my voice again and anxious for me to recount the events that had occurred since we last spoke. By then I was clean-shaven and properly clothed. We met downstairs for tea. I shared my adventures in and around Varanasi, Kushinagar, and Lumbini.

I recounted my clearly impetuous and hair-raising but amusing exploits driving to Kushinagar from Varanasi with a paan-chewing driver while avoiding Tata lorries and elephant rear ends. Both of Amit's eyebrows rose. I expressed to him how amused I was to have continued north until we crossed the border into Nepal.

"That wasn't part of the plan when I left here a few weeks ago, that's for sure!" I said with a thrilled look in my eyes.

"Indeed, Mr. Sibilla," Amit confirmed, "that wasn't discussed, but I am delighted at your safe return to the Imperial! Why did you decide to go to Nepal in the first place, if I might ask?"

"Because my Tibetan monk friend, Tenzin Kalsang B, said it was, in his words, *close*." For some reason when I said that out loud to Amit, it sounded a bit silly. I hadn't even questioned Tenzin Kalsang B about what he understood the word *close* to mean. I'm certain Amit would not have considered a drive of 350 kilometers along the north Indian country roadways "close" by any interpretation of that word.

The flawlessly dressed Amit smiled politely as he sat across from me, visibly stunned by my nerve at traversing India without so much as a map. I thanked him for all of his help, as I was set to depart India the next day, promising to return soon.

A few years later, I did return to the Imperial Hotel, this time seeking the assistance of Mohit, assistant manager and concierge.

In the interim years, Tenzin Kalsang B and I corresponded by mail and later by e-mail via the Internet café that had opened for business near the monastery. A man of my word, I came back to India to visit with him in Dharamsala.

I arranged a convenient time to meet with Mohit. At the appointed time, I introduced myself, although he apparently had been briefed by the front desk staff, the concierge staff, or both regarding who I was.

"Good morning," I began with a smile. "I need to fulfill a promise I made several years ago to my monk friend who lives in Dharamsala with the Dalai Lama. Can you help me?"

Without blinking an eye, he responded with all of the professionalism I had come to expect of a representative of the Imperial Hotel.

"A pleasure!" Mohit declared. "I will see what kind of *shhed-dule* we can put together for you. Now let me gather some details." There was nothing more elegant in my mind than listening to this perfectly appointed Indian gentleman pronounce *schedule* as two words.

"Lovely!" I said, channeling my inner Brit. "I'll be here for a few days, but let's see what you can do to get me to Dharamsala by, say, the week's end? However—trains, planes, cars—I'm good!"

Later that day, Mohit arranged for transportation to take me to and from the railway station. I had negotiated it before and assured him I could purchase passage on my own if he gave me the departure information. Not one to question a guest's request, he did so in spite of meeting my confidence that I could do so on my own with a fair degree of skepticism.

There was good reason for his concern. Suffice it to say that the New Delhi Railway Station was the most congested station in perhaps all of India, handling nearly four hundred trains with sixteen tracks and half a million passengers each day. With Mohit's help shuttling me to and from the hotel, and notwithstanding my being in the wrong queue for about thirty minutes, I eventually came face-to-face with Mr. J. J. Meena of the Indian Railway System (IRS).

J.J. was elderly, modestly dressed, and clearly a career employee with a personality that probably denied him the much sought-after Employee of the Month award. He wasn't mean-spirited. He simply trudged along quietly and resourcefully. While waiting in the wrong queue, I had time to prepare my departure form based upon Mohit's notes.

J.J. eventually waved me over to his desk. He sat next to another IRS clerk who was a Sikh with a beautifully fitted turban and sporting an immaculately groomed beard and moustache. I handed J.J. my form. He gave it the once-over and then he began to enter my information into his computer. I watched as he poked at his keyboard with his right-hand index finger as if it were the eye of a shark and he was defending himself from an attack.

Station:

> Click. *P.*
> Click. *A.*
> Click. *T.*
> Click. *H.*
> Click. *A.*
> Click. *N.*
> Click. *K.*
> Click. *O.*
> Click. *T.*

Train no.:

> Click. *4.*
> Click. *0.*
> Click. *3.*
> Click. *3.*

Kilometers:

> Click. *4.*
> Click. *8.*
> Click. *5.*

And so it went.

Much later that day, J.J. handed me a piece of paper entitled "Journey Cum Reservation Ticket." For those of you unfamiliar with early nineteenth-century prepositions, *cum* means "with" or "related by function," such as in "couch-cum-sleeper-bed." I paid him the fare totaling INR881 (about US$18), thinking the transaction was over.

Not today. J.J. held the ticket up to the light and then made it a point to review with me every detail of my pending journey.

"Second-class passage."

"Coach, A1."

"Upper berth."

"Jammu Mail no. 4033."

"Pathankot Station."

J.J. showed me my departure time and arrival time. He read the refund policy if I missed the train. He read the policy on baggage. He read ... *everything.*

To his credit, J.J. ensured there were no misunderstandings between the Indian Railway System and me. He took his time as if I were the last passenger in the entirety of the Indian railway world. And yes, he also took my time. But I took comfort in Rushdie's observation, so I just let it go. *All things in their own time,* I assured myself, realizing I was presently trapped somewhere between yesterday and tomorrow.

But in a world infested with recorded messages, endless telephone prompts, and live chats, I confess that I found it refreshing, on some level, to speak with someone in customer service while sitting in front of my interlocutor. I could see that the man who was helping me wasn't just old. J.J. was old school, like a kind uncle who explains with excruciating minutiae how to bait a hook on a fishing pole when all you want to do is drop the line into the water as fast as you can and begin fishing. You loved that uncle. And like that kind uncle, in the next instant I wanted to ring J.J.'s neck.

When J.J. finally handed me my ticket, as fast as you could say,

"Bob's your uncle and Nellie's your aunt!" I sprinted out of there. Back at the Imperial Hotel, I gathered my things together, left some belongings with the bell desk, grabbed some food, and a took a much needed nap before my all-night train departed.

FROM DHARAMSALA TO JAISALMER

That was story behind how I had come to be on an all-night train on Friday the thirteenth. I shared my sleeper car with Mohan, a polite older gentleman. When I entered the compartment, he greeted me warmly, offered tea before sleep, and then tucked himself away for the night.

The following morning, I shared a cup of chai with him that we bought from the tea wallah. Mohan was a businessman from Mumbai who was headed to the disputed territory of Jammu-Kashmir in the north to handle some family matters. Even though India and Pakistan had been warring over Jammu-Kashmir for over fifty years, the clear and present danger of violence did not seem to worry him as much as it did me.

In the course of our conversation, Mohan told me that he had been born in Rajasthan. His smile betrayed the happy memories from his boyhood.

"Mr. Guy," he began, "you must go to Rajasthan and see the Golden City of Jaisalmer. The books call it the 'Land of the Kings,' but it is special, my home, for its people."

I was drawn to the notion that as breathtaking as the Golden City of Jaisalmer eventually proved itself to be, for Mohan it was more than just the beautiful stones. People are the real treasure of a place. Buildings may be magnificent in and of themselves, but memorable stories are rarely about bricks and mortar.

Tales worth telling always center on people, like Chief Guendon of Lomé, République Togolaise. He taught me what good voodoo is and what bad voodoo can do. Or Mohammed Muhraddin, a painter from Baghdad living in Jordan whose name means "Horse of God," and who taught me how much fun it is to eat lamb kabobs, drink vodka, and smoke *nargeilah* in Amman. And President Kay Rala Xanana Gusmão of Timor-Leste, commander of the Falintil rebel forces who reminded me to cherish the freedoms he nearly died fighting for.

My chance encounter with Mohan was just the most recent of an endless string of fortuitous meetings I have enjoyed during my years of travel. Honestly, meeting so many compassionate, helpful, interesting people was a recurring, somewhat inexplicable experience.

Then, one day I met an Indian professor of business administration who was teaching in the Amman. We were staying at the same hotel, and I noticed that each morning he arrived and ate alone. One morning while breakfast was being served, I waved at him and invited him to share my table. As did the novelist Edith Wharton, I have found that travel reveals just how many good, kind people there are in the world.

He was from Delhi, sported a coat and tie, and had a quick wit. Soon, we were laughing. I expressed that I was continually charmed to meet such remarkable people like him, no matter how far from home I strayed. I thanked him for a brilliant breakfast. Before we parted, he left me with this story:

> A sadhu, an Indian holy man, was sitting on the side of the road when a young man pulling a cart of personal belongings approached him. The young man explained that he was from a faraway village but had left because there was no work. He pointed at the lights in the distance and asked the sadhu, "Do you see that village? Do you know what kind of people live there?"
>
> The sadhu looked up and asked the young boy, "What kind of people are in your village?"

Without hesitating, the young man said, "I am happy to leave there, as they are nasty people who talk behind your back, tell lies, and never lend a helping hand!"

The sadhu looked at the young man and said, "They are the same kind of people!" The young man left disappointed.

A little later, another young man pulling a cart of personal belongings approached the sadhu. The young man explained that he was from a far-off village but had left in search of work. He pointed at the lights in the distance and asked the sadhu, "Do you see that village? Do you know what kind of people live there?"

The sadhu looked up and asked the young boy, "What kind of people are in your village?"

The young man replied, "I already miss my family and friends. They are considerate and caring and always ready to help anyone in need."

The sadhu looked at the young man and said, "They are the same kind of people!"

With that memory in mind and with a nod to fate, I pledged to Mohan, "After I visit with my friend Tenzin Kalsang B in Dharamsala, I will go to Rajasthan. Thank you so very much for your thoughtfulness." Just as Tenzin Kalsang B had put me on the road to Lumbini, Mohan had pointed me in the direction of Jailsalmer. Once again, I would be off to see what I could see.

At Pathankot Station, I found a car for hire to drive me the 90 kilometers to Dharamsala. After nearly three hours of twists and turns into the hills, I came upon Glenmoor Cottages in Upper Dharamsala. I met with a very accommodating desk clerk, Ajai, and was quickly inside my room resting.

Before I retired, though, I asked Ajai if there was any way he could get a message to Namgyal Monastery and my friend Tenzin Kalsang B.

"Yes, sir!" Ajai replied enthusiastically. "I will take care of that for you, sir. Please rest now!"

In about an hour or so, I watched as a smiling monk in his saffron- and maroon-colored robe bounded uphill to greet me. It was a joyful reunion with my friend. Unlike the plains far below, here the air was cool and crisp. We sat for tea on the front lawn.

It had been three years since we last saw each other.

Dharamsala served as the home of the Dalai Lama, and as the provisional Tibetan government for millions of refugees. In 1950, China initiated its military occupation of the Tibetan Plateau. Since then, hundreds of thousands of Tibetans have died under Chinese rule, which has also forced Tenzin Kalsang B and millions of his fellow countrymen and countrywomen to live as refugees in Nepal, India, and Bangladesh. So it came as no surprise as we walked the streets of Dharamsala to see shuttered doorways smacked with placards demanding that China "Get Out of Tibet!" and "Free Tibet!"

Tenzin Kalsang B lived at the end of a long walkway on the second level of a five-level concrete structure. If there had been a contest to design an ugly, dull, uninspired monastery, this building would have won the Jury Prize for Excellence in the Unimaginative Architecture Category. It was little more than a large rectangle into which smaller rectangular rooms had been carved. There was no in-room plumbing. There was no in-room heating system. It was a Motel 6 from hell.

By my estimate, Tenzin Kalsang B's room was eight feet wide and fourteen feet long. Because it was at the end of the hall, the room was slightly larger than the others. He gladly shared his room with another monk. In fact, his roommate was so tall that Tenzin Kalsang B slept widthwise so his roommate could sleep lengthwise. That may also explain why there wasn't any furniture.

The room did have two small windows. From the middle of the ceiling, a bare light bulb dangled from a wire that obviously had not been installed by a licensed electrician.

On our way out, Tenzin Kalsang B showed me where he "hid" the key to his door so I might enter if he was still at class or *puja* (prayer). He confided that pretty much everyone knew where his key was. Besides, the key hung in clear view on a string suspended to the left and above the doorway.

I was surprised that there were locks on the doors in that building. In the end, perhaps it wasn't such a bad idea given the fact that the only thing keeping unwanted people out of the monastery grounds was one rather small sign that warned, No Visitors Allowed After Dark.

I awoke the next morning at the cottages to the bugling of the Tibetan long trumpet, the *dungchen*, which began inexplicably each day at 5:00 a.m. At dawn, the monks from nearby Kirti Jaepa Monastery sent the slightly melancholy guttural base tones into the valley below. It was as if a huge ship had somehow made its way up through five thousand feet and let off a blow of its foghorn. Accompanying the deep reverberation was the scratchy timbre of the *gyaling*, the dungchen's shorter and shriller cousin. But it was all pleasantly resonant, even at such an ungodly hour of the morning.

As the days passed, it was apparent to me that neither the Dalai Lama nor his followers lived in a bubble. Tenzin Kalsang B and his friends may be monks, but that does not make them monastic in the stereotypical sense of that term. They are in no way sequestered from the creep of commercial culture and do not repudiate it. In fact, just the opposite is true.

A community infused with traces of Western commerce encircled Tenzin Kalsang B. Pepsi marketed bottled water with its trademark red, white, and blue disc on the label. One local competitor packaged *Panihari*, which has a sketch of an Indian woman balancing clay water pots on her head. With the proximity of the highest mountain chain on earth a mere border crossing away, it came as no surprise that water bottled and sold by the Everest Mineral Water Ltd. is marketed under the label *Himalayan*. My personal favorite was called Mr. Cool.

Several restaurants advertised pizza and cappuccino, but caveat emptor should guide your decision. And fronting what may loosely be described as the town square, a video house promoted a showing of *Spiderman*.

"I very like this movie *Spiderman*!" Tenzin Kalsang B exclaimed excitedly. Holy meets Hollywood.

Magazines, newspapers, videos, CDs, and satellite television bombarded the monks daily with today's modern lifestyle of instant gratification. Fast food. Computers. Cell phones. The monastery even had a small TV room.

"Many monks making much shouting!" Tenzin Kalsang B reported during soccer season, rolling his eyes.

Tenzin Kalsang B eagerly admitted to liking the same kinds of things many Americans do: pizza, Pepsi, and chocolate. After he received a package from me from Honolulu, he once wrote the following (in his own words and letters):

> Hear I am happy to receive your affectionate letter
> with T-shirt and the card of your homeland. I like
> card very much. And also chocolate. Me and my
> friends eat the chocolate together ... we all like it so
> thanks a lots.

It became our ritual of sorts. I sent chocolate with a letter, and he always told me how much he and his friends enjoyed it. How we communicated evolved over time, however.

On occasion, he used to cross Temple Road just beyond the

monastery gates to go to the Internet café. Diagonally across the potholed road fronting the unattractive monastery was an equally unattractive two-story concrete structure painted sky blue. Above the doorway, a notice set the fare at "10 rupees" (about US20¢) "for ten minutes."

I entered with a twinge of resignation. Just when I thought I had seen it all, I walked into a room full of monks hunched over computer screens with shaved heads and fingers extending out from maroon robes eagerly logging on during a break from their classes. They were sending e-mails, surfing the Net, and doing all of the things people all over the world do on their computers. Buddhist lesson no. 3: We are not as different from one another as we might appear.

Tenzin Kalsang B embraced the new technology as enthusiastically as anyone. Still, some traditions hung on. Like his letters, his e-mails always began with "Tashi delak!"—a Tibetan expression of greeting and blessing. Actually, in his e-mails he also included an expression from Hawaii:

> Hi many aloha n tashidelak from ur friend,,here I get ur reply n feel very happy to know that u r comng here soon,, as u had wrote that u will be coming after nepal, lets me know how long you will be in nepal?/? after nepal I guess u r coming to delhi right? Then by bus to dharamsala right?

Like everyone, I suppose, there are times I long for the past. The tradition of posting missives from abroad was not ever better illustrated than in *The Original Letters from India* (1908) by Mrs. Eliza Fay. She was a dedicated writer even while jailed. I can't conceive of how long and by what manner her letters from Calcutta to London would have made their way, but they did.

Even if I whined that one of my letters took six weeks to be delivered, it always, miraculously, dependably, unfailingly arrived at the desk of the Mail Monk, from whom Tenzin Kalsang B was happy to receive it. Especially the chocolates.

Now, sometimes I just hit Send.

It's not the same.

One of the surprising things about spending time with Tenzin Kalsang B was seeing how normal a twenty-something-year-old he was. One sunny afternoon, Tenzin Kalsang B took me for a swim at Baghsu Falls, a favorite place of many of the monks. We made our way to the edge of town where the buildings yielded to the lush forest green of the mountains and high white clouds. When I looked up past the cloud line, I saw icy snowcapped mountains. I knew then exactly how cold the water was going to be.

There, amid the laughter and chattering teeth, we became a living rainbow. Baghsu Falls was packed with half-clothed student monks and me. Our brown skin appeared the color of coffee as we bathed in our white underwear. Maroon and saffron piles of clothes lay scattered on the ground. We submerged ourselves in opaque water the color of dark avocado. And we jumped around freezing with blue lips and jet-black hair.

When I thanked him for going to all of the trouble to be excused from school to take me swimming, he smirked.

"What?" I asked, both of my hands outstretched.

"I tell Attendance Monk I am sick!" Tenzin Kalsang B said. Then his contagious laughter began.

"Attendance Monk say many monks sick today. Must be weather is good!" he declared, laughing even more loudly now.

For all of his joking, Tenzin Kalsang B had been a devoted student for over fourteen years. At the conclusion of one year's study, he was declared first in his class and for that distinction was awarded a purse of twenty-five rupees (about fifty cents in US money). For his dedication to the daily rituals of prayer, study, and monastic chores, he collected a monthly stipend of INR200 (roughly US$4.25). Tenzin Kalsang B was not in it for the money.

Time in north India, mystifyingly, seemed to move both faster and slower than in most other places I've been in the world. There were days like the one at Baghsu Falls when the simple joy of life at play in cold water and drinking hot chai afterward somehow tricked me into believing that days as good as those would never end.

Then there were days when I recalled actually watching the sun slide inexorably from east to west as if time-lapse photography had collapsed the entire process into three or four fleeting moments.

Much too soon, Tenzin Kalsang B and I were once again bidding each other farewell. Before I left, he gave me a string of prayer flags as a gift and told me to suspend them above my house. Each color signified the natural environment: yellow for earth, white for air, red for fire, green for water, and blue for sky.

"Hang wind horse above home," he advised. "It bring good blessings to you and your family."

That's how my friend Tenzin Kalsang B thought. He believed in the protective power of prayer and, because of this, believed that life did not have to be one long struggle in the dark.

Sometimes, though, our struggles were in the daylight. Like when I missed the train back to Delhi. Shit happens. No one kept track of time here at the end of the clouds. The days were divided into daytime and nighttime, and calendars didn't go well with prayer wheels or wind horse flags.

Never one to fret about spilled milk, I went to the station and bought passage on a Bedi Travels bus. My bus was named Potala, appropriately enough after the palace in Lhasa, Tibet, home to the Dalai Lama. The driver promised that Delhi was only fourteen *or so* hours away. I had low expectations of what the ride would be like. My expectations were diminished even further when I walked in front of the bus and saw painted across the bumper, "Oh! God Save Me!"

While en route, those proved to be the right words in the right place. From my seat, no. 13, I leaned into the aisle and watched in a state of semiparalysis as our driver approached some of the switchbacks. On the road down from the heights of Dharamsala, the hairpin turns were so narrow that several times, the bus had to stop, back up, and then complete the turn.

One slip of the foot off the brake at an inopportune moment and the trip down the mountain would have been much shorter and straighter than the itinerary proposed. An old Tibetan man sitting next to me prayed the entire way. I encouraged him with candy.

We were delayed further somewhere in the Punjab at 1:36 a.m. by a jeep full of Sikh police. They pulled the bus over, and our driver exited to speak with each of the officers. Soon, a bunch of us also exited the bus to stretch our legs. An impeccably dressed Nepalese man standing next to me offered an explanation after I asked him if he had any idea what the problem was. He smiled and said calmly, "I think we must pay the compensation."

And there it was, the ubiquitous and shameless presence of baksheesh. Other delays compounded the earlier delays, until I began to repeat the words on the front bumper to myself like a mantra: "Oh! God save me!"

It didn't work.

Or maybe it did. My estimated fourteen-hour ride to central Delhi arrived twelve hours late. But we arrived.

Without sounding too new age, I found it worthy of recording in my journal that I had left Delhi for Dharamsala on Friday the thirteenth and that my return bus seat was no. 13. This mathematical symmetry demanded contemplation over a gin martini or two, which would occur immediately upon my arrival at the Imperial Hotel, no matter what time of day or night that might be.

I hoped I wasn't making too much of all this. The traffic light at an intersection in New Delhi suggested an answer as it flashed the word *RELAX* across the face of the red light while our engine idled.

I wanted to relax, but I couldn't. Even before I had arrived for a shower, a shave, and some rest within the serenity of the Imperial Hotel, I had already begun to consider arrangements for my departure to Rajasthan and the Golden City of Jaisalmer.

When I opened the door to my room, the belongings I had left with the bell desk had already been delivered, my books placed onto the writing desk, and my clean clothes hanging in the closet. I walked over and thumbed through my well-worn copy of "Endymion" by John Keats, a poem that has accompanied me on virtually every journey I have taken in my adult life.

Whether I was climbing the Western Breach wall of Mt. Kilimanjaro, or trekking the snowy Italian Dolomites near Cortina, or traversing the jungles of Belize and Guatemala, "Endymion" came with me. And now it was coming with me into Rajasthan's Thar Desert.

Keats observed, after all of Endymion's travels, "Yet for him there's refreshment even in toil." I too was one for the road with all of its struggles. Beginning to plan my way back out before I had even washed the dust of the Punjab plains off of my face, I picked up the phone and left a message with Mohit.

The next morning, a note that had been slipped under my door read, "Please see the assistant manager in charge of concierge services today at your convenience." I was home.

We met at his desk. Mohit politely asked me about my trip to Dharamsala. I recounted my journey there and the slightly harrowing return in some detail. "Oh! God save me!" I exclaimed with dramatic emphasis.

He was bemused.

"That's nothing compared to my last trip to Varanasi, Kushinagar, and Lumbini," I avowed. I essentially retold him what I had said to his colleague Amit a few years earlier. He looked at me like a third eye had, in fact, appeared on my forehead.

"Mohit, may I count on your assistance to help me with arrangements to Jaisalmer?" I finished, channeling my inner Brit.

"Of course, Mr. Sibilla!" Mohit exclaimed with a slight bobble of the head. "Perhaps you wish to rest another day or so to gather your strength? It seems you have been through quite a lot since you last departed the Imperial."

Indeed. The following day, I was taken by taxi to a travel agency located "behind Shiela Cinema," had paid INR11,065 (about US$235) for my airfare, and began preparations for departure in the direction of the setting sun. I would fly to Jodhpur, the Blue City, known for the vast number of homes painted sacred blue in honor of the god Shiva.

Jodhpur was nearly 300 kilometers from Jaisalmer. Since I had never been to Jodhpur, I decided that before I grabbed a train to Jaisalmer, I would hang out there for a few days.

The memory of Mohit bidding me farewell was still fresh as I stepped out of the airport at Jodhpur. There I was greeted immediately by two of my most familiar travel companions: dust and confusion. The now familiar mayhem was as it always was in India. I was besieged immediately by shoeless young boys who should have been in school instead of tugging at my clothes and chasing me down for rupees.

"Hello, sir!"

"Where are you from?"

"Do you have a pen?"

"Where is your hotel?"

"How long do you stay?"

It goes without saying, but different people handle bedlam differently. Some fear these waist-high mobs no matter how often they are confronted by them in India. They get frustrated by the unwelcome intrusion. They try to repel the unwanted touching. Unrealistically, they want quiet in a very unquiet country. And in the end, some people react … *unpleasantly*, shall we say?

Personally, I like kids. And putting myself in their place, I am quite certain they would rather be playing than bothering me for a few rupees. India, though, is a poor country and everyone has to do what he or she must. Instead of responding in fear or anger, I deployed a little child psychology: I paid attention to them. And at the appropriate time, I used misdirection. When a kid asked, "Sir, where are you from?" I would look him or her in the eye and ask,

"Where are *you* from?" The usual result was a blank look. Wasn't I the one who had just gotten off the plane?

When one asked, "Sir, do you have a pen?" I would say simply, "Yes I do." And I smiled a lot. I joked with them. I teased them. And then I would reach into my pocket, hand the tallest kid I saw a fistful of candy, and tell him (or her) to pass it around. While the children pounced on one of their own, I would run in the opposite direction.

In this case, luckily I ended up running into the Hotel Haveli Guest House and also into Upendra, the front desk clerk. He greeted me with so much enthusiasm that I felt like I was his only guest. Maybe I was. My room was simple, clean, and forgettable. However, the view from the rooftop restaurant was anything but. I have rarely seen anything as enormous and equally majestic as the panoramic display of the Mehrangarh Fort. Rudyard Kipling described it as being the work of "angels, fairies and giants." This may sound bizarre, but at night when they light up this fifteenth-century desert fortress, it is like the entire hill is suspended by fireflies.

While meandering through the grounds in and around the Mehrangarh Fort, I met Sanjay, who acted as my guide. We discussed the history of the region as we strolled past women in burqas and through Saracenic archways. We walked by a cannon still pointed threateningly across the landscape of blue homes. He told me how a maharaja named Jodha had merged his name with *pur*, which means "city," giving the city its name, Jodhpur.

But Jodhpur is not Jaisalmer. Later that week, I jumped onto a train departing at 11:15 p.m. for another all-night ride, this one to Jaisalmer.

An estimated 11 million people daily are moved cheaply and efficiently to 7,085 different destinations in India by rail. For less than US$10, I enjoyed first-class passage between Jodhpur and Jaisalmer. The Indian railway did not discriminate Hindu from Muslim or Jain from Sikh. Or wayward Japanese-Italian wanderers. The trains were how all of India, plus me, moved.

"I am here in the season of the drought and full moon," I

scribbled in my journal, after managing to find my sleeper car. I was also here during military maneuvers, lying faceup in a sleeper car filled with Indian soldiers who were apparently unhappy about the prospect of spending a year in the desert guarding India's western frontier.

The next morning I stepped onto a dusty platform and saw a camel pulling a cart. I knew then that I had gone farther than the 300 kilometers indicated on my map. My train had also served as a time machine.

There were men calling in tongues not derived from Latin. They wore turbans, *lunghis*, and dhotis. Hindu women were dressed in gloriously colored saris, and Muslim women wore burqas.

Jain temples, Hindu shrines, and Islamic mosques were all built within praying distance of one another. Cattle, considered holy by the Hindus, wandered the streets freely. This was what civilization looked like after several thousand years.

With a modest amount of effort, I found a room at the Desert Haveli, a five-hundred-year-old sandstone building. The house was roughly square and three stories high. The main entranceway was so low that even at 5'6" I had to bend down to keep from banging my head.

As soon as I stood erect, Hari came over to welcome me. I asked if I could get a room for week or so, preferably with a window looking out into the desert. Little did I know that all of their rooms had windows, as that was the primary source of air and light. Maybe I did bang my head, as I seemed to have forgotten that this building was five hundred years old and not likely to have been retrofitted with interior lighting. With that, I began my life in the Golden City of Jaisalmer.

The center of the *haveli* opened straight up into the sky. It was an efficient way to vent heat from the building. I arose early one morning and wandered up to the covered portion of the rooftop, which also served as the eating area. As dawn broke, I could see people sleeping on the flat tops of buildings all across the city. In the cool night air and with the stars as a ceiling, I realized the locals reserved the best rooms for themselves.

Back in the spring of 1155, a Bhati Rajput king named Jaisal consulted a holy man to assist in selecting the location for his fort. The sadhu gave his blessing to a site on top of a triangular plateau; it was here that the walls of the citadel were built. Merging the word *meru*, which means "hill," with his own name, the place became known as Jaisalmer.

The parapets of the fort are made of sandstone block quarried from what once was the bottom of an endless Paleolithic sea. As a consequence, the huge ramparts, which soar above the desert floor, create the rising image of a massive dune instead of an impregnable stronghold.

The battlements cling to the edge of an indiscriminate escarpment, extending inward and outward as if they are the legs of some gigantic creature. Its walls rise like the tail of a scorpion, curved and not entirely vertical. It leans slightly inward with each successive, superior stone. Looking outward from my window, I could only imagine how indebted those who lived within these fortress walls must have felt to their protective king.

"Sir, from where do you come?" I heard being shouted from behind me one day while wandering the narrow alleyway leading to my haveli. I turned in the direction of a young boy and greeted him with a smile.

"I am from Hawaii," I answered.

"Hawa?" he asked as he tilted his head slightly and squinted through both of his big round Hindu eyes.

"Hawa?" he repeated a moment later, with the quizzical look on his face that transcended international and cultural boundaries.

"Yes, I'm from Hawa," I replied, granting him some elbow room on the pronunciation.

He hesitated.

"But sir, what country do you come from?" he implored once again.

I learned later that day from Hari that the Hindi word *hawa* means "wind." In the charm and garble that sometimes occurs when languages collided, apparently I had told the young boy I was "from the wind."

That sounded about right to me. It confirmed that the poetry of life is scattered around us every day, everywhere. It is not hidden away like the pelagic fish of the deep sea. It is more like the colorful and playful reef fish that require only that we take the time to look at them to see their beauty.

While I might have come with the wind, some Rajasthanis came by camel. I awakened every day to the sight of dromedaries. One morning over a cup of chai, a local camel driver named Majeed explained to me how the dromedary got its hump. There is biology, and then there is suspension of disbelief. This story was clearly leaning toward the latter. I was intrigued.

"A long time ago ..." he began.

I smiled. In this place that had been occupied for thousands of years, everything must have begun "a long time ago."

"Shiva, the Creator," he continued, "was married to Parvati. One day, Parvati asked her husband for a beast to help her carry her things. Shiva fashioned for her a five-legged animal. Shiva breathed life into it by blowing the word *unth* into its mouth."

I looked confused.

"*Unth*," he explained, "is Hindi for 'camel.'"

"Got it."

"The beast rose, but was unable to walk because it had too many legs. Shiva saw the problem, reached over, tore one of the legs from its body, and shoved it back into the unth. Since then, the camel has had a hump."

"Maybe that is why people say they are such difficult animals?" I suggested, laughing approvingly at his story.

I learned also that Rajasthanis are a proud people.

"It is custom for Rajasthani men to wear a *pagdi*," Majeed explained, "mostly red, yellow, and orange turbans."

I mentioned I had seen many men with orange turbans.

"Men friends will promise forever friendship by exchanging their turbans," Majeed explained. In fact, he continued, a pagdi is such an important part of a man's status that "if a man places his turban at the feet of another, it is the most sincere gesture of apology a Rajasthani man can make."

"I can't imagine so much significance is placed on a man's cloth," I said in dismay.

"Exactly!" confirmed Majeed. "A man's pagdi is so valuable, he can even borrow money by promising his turban to ensure repayment."

After everything Majeed had said, it occurred to me that he wasn't really talking about the turban. It wasn't the pagdi itself. The turban was merely a symbol of the promise of one Rajasthani man to another. As modest as the actual value of the cloth of the pagdi may be, it embodied the immeasurable valuable of a man's word. Some traditions are worth keeping.

I awakened in my haveli on the morning of my departure back to Delhi and scribbled some notes before I got back on the road. India had taught me to grab poetry from the air around me. It revealed that thirteen just might be my lucky number. And it made me I question whether home was a place or simply an idea.

THE GOLDEN LAND OF FOUR MILLION PAGODAS

I woke up in Rangoon on my birthday.

It was January 16, 2002, and I was in Burma. I grabbed my bag, pulled off the luggage tag, and stuck the evidence in my journal: "Yangon Myan, 16 Jan., RGN Thai Airways 303." In 1989 the ruling military junta changed the name of their country from Burma to Myanmar, but I couldn't resist calling it by its exotic colonial name. I'm old school, and I was getting one year older today.

It took some doing to get here. I transited through Tokyo to Bangkok. The six-hour layover in Thailand was too brief for a hotel room and too long to stay sober. So I stumbled into the Bentley Pub on the fourth floor of the now closed Don Mueang International Airport and ordered a gin martini.

When I sat down, it was 12:04 a.m. and the place was full of Caucasian men with their wives. Or Thai girlfriends. Or perhaps both. They didn't call it Bangkok for nothing. I drank through the drone of announcements: Phnom Penh Airlines; Kazakhstan Airlines; Royal Brunei Airlines; El Al Israel Airlines; Aeroflot Russian Airlines; Air Niugini; Cameroon Airlines; Merpati Nusantara Airlines; Qatar Airways. The names kept coming, and so did my gin martinis.

"Sir, we will be landing soon. Please bring your chair upright and fasten your seatbelt!" was the next thing I remembered. The slight pressure of a tiny hand and a soft voice brought me to awareness. Groggy-eyed, I looked outside and watched as a sprawling city rose up from the ground. When the wheels chirped onto the runway, it was my birthday and I was in Rangoon.

I had no plan or language skills for Myanmar. I simply wanted to be gone for my birthday, away from friends, family, and any other potential well-wishers.

Over time, my birthday had evolved into a private affair. No cake. No candles. No "Happy Birthday to You" renditions.

For me, each birthday demanded private reflection. Without sounding too glum, over the last thirty years, I have made it a point to regularly update my own obituary. With each revision, I mention things I did, add things I desire to do, and sometimes include my thoughts on what I hope to do, hope to become, and hope to achieve until the next revision.

It isn't a bucket list. That is too sullen. Instead, I want to identify and then satisfy my desires while alive enough to do so: discovering the elation of climbing Swiss mountains in the early years as a Boy Scout in Germany; learning that my size meant I was better as the president of the Literature Club in high school than as quarterback of the football team; finding out that when I recited poetry, it became sexier to girls the older I got; changing employment after matriculating from the College of William and Mary in Virginia; changing my career choice after three years of graduate school; searching for a greater understanding of what a life of *value* looked like; finding love in my lifetime and then embracing its loss with wonder equal to its discovery; and sensing the pure joy of the freedom to move across the earth and learning from strangers.

Writing my obituary forces me to assess how I am living my life while I am in the middle of it. In *The Curious Case of Benjamin Button*, F. Scott Fitzgerald observes that while we all live our lives going forward, we really only understand our life when looking backward. My autobiographical, ever-evolving, self-edited obituary allows me to do both.

I look at the past to help guide my future. At the same time,

I look toward the future knowing it will soon be in my rearview mirror. My obituary makes me Benjamin Button.

I don't suffer from any internal drama when I join in the merriment for someone else's birthday. I view every day as my birthday and far too often act like it. I have been known to order a gin martini at lunch knowing a nap is soon to follow. Or watch a foreign film on a Thursday afternoon. Or buy a friend a gift for no reason at all.

Sometimes I get dealt sixes, sevens, and eights just like everyone does. People I know and love and cherish get sick, get into accidents, and sometimes die, even as my birthdays keep mounting. Whoever wrote, "Statistics have shown that those who have the most birthdays tend to live the longest," wasn't viewing life the way I do. Instead, I identify with Robert Frost's idealistic assessment that "happiness makes up in height what it lacks in length." Length for its own sake is overrated.

For me, this day, this 1/365th of the year, was special. Even though I could've been anywhere else, I found myself waking up in this very extraordinary place. Intentionality is what they call it now.

Thus, in the Year of the Snake, I came to spend my birthday in Rangoon of the Republic of the Union of Myanmar. By the way, in Myanmar, Wednesday is split, with the morning being Black Elephant Day and the afternoon being White Elephant Day. Since my birthday landed on a Wednesday, I had inherited the right to a celebration that lasted for two days.

Outside of baggage claim, I was drawn immediately to a sign that wanted my business: New Place Travels – Carrying out tour operation toward your's satisfactory [sic]. A very slight young Burmese woman with dazzling long black hair manned the desk.

Just before I began to speak, I realized I didn't know how to say hello in Burmese.

"Minga lau bah!" she said with a bright smile. "Can I help you, sir?"

"Yes!" I exclaimed, delighted by her English. That fact alone reminded me that this had been a British colony for over 125 years and was given its independence just after World War II.

"Where do you wish to go?" she inquired.

There it was again. I was in a city in a foreign country, and I had no roof and no solutions.

Arriving with a plan rarely had been my approach to international travel. I usually headed off with only a vague notion of where I wanted to go, and how I was going to get there once I figured out where there was. When I was going to return was an added mystery. And where to stay. And how to get around. And all of the other questions in between.

"Sorry, miss," I said, knowing I was now placing myself in her hands, "any suggestions?"

She thought for a second and then offered, "I can recommended the Three Seasons Hotel."

I thought the same thing.

"The *Three* Seasons Hotel?" I repeated slowly for confirmation.

"Yes, sir! I know that it you will like. With certainty, sir."

Nod of the head.

I confess she had me at *Minga lau bah*!

"Okay! The Three Seasons it is!" I replied, even though I heard myself saying *Four* in my head. I wondered what *Three* was going to get me.

"Your passport, please? And your FEC [foreign exchange certificate] voucher, thank you!" she asked with efficiency.

Kay Kay was her name, and it was apropos because her name referred to her long black hair. What she had asked for was a way for the Republic of the Union of Myanmar to get hard currency by requiring every tourist who arrived to convert at least two hundred US dollars into FECs (pronounced "fecks"). This was a one-way transaction. Only FECs above US$200 could be changed back to US dollars. This was a tax in the form of a money exchange. The problem was that you couldn't dump FECs onto a campfire. Most travelers to Myanmar considered FECs worthless unless they stayed at approved Western hotels.

After buying the minimum number of FECs, I also bought kyats (pronounced "chats"), the money that moved the local economy.

I handed my FEC voucher to Kay Kay, which stated the following, politely:

> KINDLY NOTE that it is compulsory for FIT and FV
> to exchange US$200 with FEC.
> For reconversion, only the excess of US$200 will be allowed.
> Yangon Foreign Trade Bank

As an aside, the government of Myanmar apparently knew me better than some of my friends did. The powers that ruled here classified me as a FIT: a foreign independent traveler. I could not have described myself any better if I tried. But to Myanmar, it meant simply that I was not part of a group of ten or more. As always, I was on my own.

I assumed the FV designation was for "foreign visitors." Regardless, I was soon to have two hundred US dollars less than I'd had a few minutes ago.

The rate was US$1 to 1 FEC. Kay Kay completed a form on New Place Travels letterhead that affirmed proudly, "In Co-operated [sic] With Myanmar Airport Limousine Services Co., Ltd." On it, she wrote, "Destination: Three Seasons Hotel"; then, "Date: 16.01"; and finally, "Time: 10:40." This seemed like a lot of paperwork for a ride, but how this country operated was a blank space in my mind.

I gave her 5 FECs and then off I sped in an un-air-conditioned four-door Toyota Corolla that served as my "limousine" driven by a young Burmese man who had clearly failed to show up for his driving test. Having no concept of what Rangoon was as a city, everything fascinated me as we zoomed by.

We rounded the enormous shimmering gold dome of the mystical Shwedagon Pagoda as we raced south. Moist, hot tropical air blew in from the rear window as we sped along much too fast for the congestion on the roadway. There were people on bicycles hauling goods balanced (to my mind) impossibly and precariously. Other cyclists were pumping away madly on tricycles as passengers sat restfully in the shaded rickshaw.

Trucks and cars wound in front of and behind us without regard to lanes or markings on the roadway. Horns created a fugue of un-syncopated melodies. Men and women wore fabrics with colors that bore no relationship to the color swatches for, say, the Behr paint you might find at Home Depot. Clothing patterns went in every direction. This was chaos in full visual and sonic display.

As you might imagine, the air coming into the backseat from the open window provided little relief from the tropical heat. We turned east before Monkey Point, and somewhere between the Free Bird Travel Agency and the East Yangon General Hospital, we pulled up, rather sweaty I might add, to a sign with "Three Seasons" displayed vertically over "Hotel."

I've learned over the years never to judge upon first glance, as surprises, some very good ones, arise from the unfamiliar. I tipped the driver, got out of the Corolla, and walked into the lobby. At the front desk stood a stunningly pretty woman with a name suitable for a character in a Broadway play: Mimi Bo. Things were already looking up.

Arriving in Rangoon, regardless of the day, was not always good news. For the less informed, Myanmar has earned some very bad press over the last couple of decades. You may know the name Aung San Suu Kyi, the prodemocracy leader who has been placed under house arrest on and off since about 1990 by the ruling military junta. Her father, General Aung San, was famous for negotiating the 1947 treaty that gave Burma independence from Great Britain. As compensation for General Aung San's act of diplomacy and desire for a democratic Burma, the junta had him assassinated.

To be fair, Myanmar wasn't conspicuously dangerous when I dropped down from the sky into Rangoon. I went notwithstanding the fact that the US State Department had included Myanmar on its "Travel Warnings and Alerts" list. It cautioned against taking a holiday there because of the country's political instability. I thought that my destination's being declared unsafe was the best endorsement I could find to begin a good travel story.

Honestly, there were plenty of worse places. The US State Department issues at least thirty warnings annually for US citizens to avoid certain countries because of war, famine, bad weather, disease, threat of kidnapping, and other occurrences that afflict humans and their societies. Sometimes I've gone to dodgy destinations on assignment. Risky places at dicey times make for good reading.

There was that afternoon walk through one of the souks of Peshawar, Pakistan, with my camera that brought me face-to-burqa with a woman who raised her hand in the shape of a pistol, pointed it at me, and pulled the trigger. Or that time I spent with the United Nations Peacekeeping Forces from Fiji deployed in East Timor at the close of a twenty-three-year civil war with Indonesia. And then there was that weird time when three members of the Syrian secret police barged into a bedouin tent that my friend Adeeb al-Assad, Fuaz Asad, and I had taken refuge in during a sandstorm. At times, it was a threatening, weird, nonlonely planet.

Nothing even remotely like that, thank goodness, seemed to be on the horizon in Myanmar. But given the relative intolerance of Myanmar's ruling regime to Aung San Suu Kyi's demands for democratic liberty, I suspected that freedom of the press was one of those bothersome rights the junta might look upon with little, if any, humor. So I kept my plan simple: keep my notebook and camera handy but hidden, and avoid going to jail.

"Good morning!" I said to Mimi Bo with a smile. "Kay Kay sent me!" It was a private joke.

The Pazundaung township within which the Three Seasons Hotel was located was actually quite respectable and quiet in a three-star sort of way. Mimi Bo and the others who worked there could not have been more helpful, especially in helping me get out of my cargo pants and oxford cloth shirt and into something more Myanmarish.

After settling in and asking for some help with clothes, I was given a map and a few names. I suspected I was going to buy clothes from Mimi Bo's friends or family or extended family. No matter to me. I found the small store she had marked on the map.

"Minga lau bah!" an older woman inside welcomed me.

"Minga lau bah!" I said with a smile. I walked around for a minute and got down to shopping.

"May I see that longyi please?" I asked, pointing my finger. "Yes. The green one with pattern," I said, nodding my head. "And those sandals?" I asked, pointing again. "Burmese size 11," it read under the handwritten paper sign. Definitely more pointing. "And that white shirt. Do you have it in a small?"

The woman helping me motioned for me to sit down and then ran off with my longyi in hand. Soon I heard a sewing machine. When she returned, the sides of the material had been stitched together. To put it on, you step into the middle of the fabric circle, pull the fabric up to near your waist, twist the fabric into a little ball, and tuck it into your waist to keep it from unraveling. I had to practice to keep my longyi from falling to the ground as I walked back to my hotel.

My new outfit, consisting of a shirt, skirt (my term), and slippers, cost me less than US$10. I seemed to have made a striking figure. "Now you like Burmese boy!" Mimi Bo exclaimed with delight when I returned to the Three Seasons Hotel. I was already warming up to this country.

Rangoon was in full swing with the day's business. I had noticed during my walk, as Burmese men stood and talked, that they constantly tied and retied their longyis as if it were a national pastime. Along a busy sidewalk, two young ladies sat at a card table and managed a long line of customers waiting patiently to pay to use their telephone. Crowds of people darted across the chaotic streets jammed with vehicles and performed a ballet to the music of car horns. The drivers in Rangoon made it unambiguously clear that they preferred honking to braking. Interior house lights flickered incessantly as instantaneous and unpredictable power outages punctuated the rhythm of the day.

I wandered around Rangoon for a few more days. There were delightful areas of puzzlement. Take the iconic Buddhist structure in central Rangoon, the Shwedagon Pagoda. On the postcard I purchased at the airport, it was written as one word, albeit with another spelling, "Shwezigon." Then I found a two-word iteration on my map as "Shwe Dagon." My favorite version was discovered while I stopped for dinner at the Aung Yadana Restaurant. On the restaurant's card, a three-word version offered yet another, even more creative spelling, "Shwe Zi Gone."

Regardless of how you spelled the name of the pagoda, ancient invaders, colonial powers, and I couldn't help but be stunned by the imagination and commitment of the Burmese Buddhists. For twenty-five hundred years, the Shwedagon Pagoda was not merely *in* the heart of Rangoon; the Shwedagon Pagoda *was* the heart of Rangoon.

It cost US$5 for an entrance ticket, which allowed me to follow Buddhist monks in prayer. Like them, I walked around the central dome of the pagoda and in one revolution encircled the largest gold dome on earth. I smiled while circumambulating in my longyi.

I wasn't alone. Men, women, and children circled the dome clockwise in bare feet, stopping intermittently to clasp their hands together near their foreheads at altars to offer up their prayers. Some families sat together on the clean marble floor out of the path of those circling the dome, always keeping their feet pointed away from the dome, as the bottoms of the feet are considered unclean.

Monks smiled at the children and worshippers. Some sat in their red-clay-colored robes with their begging bowls in front of them awaiting patiently the kindness of others to provide for their daily sustenance. Prayer at the Shwedagon Pagoda wasn't a dreaded obligation to be fulfilled once a week. It was part of the warp and weft of Burmese life.

I always find it humorous when people speak of Buddhists

praying as if there were some grand universal set of rules for doing so. Even the simple act of praying carries with it puzzlement. For example, Tibetan Buddhists call their prayer ritual kora and, while praying, move clockwise around a religious structure.

However, when I attend the temple of my Japanese Buddhist grandparents located in Moiilili in Honolulu during *obon* season, I dance with my friends in a counterclockwise direction. For Japanese Buddhists anyway, some dance clockwise and some counterclockwise.

To non-Buddhists, the ritual of prayer seems suitably spiritual and orderly. In actuality, it is simply people walking in circles. The particular sect of Buddhism determines the direction of the journey. My point is that not all things are as divine as they appear.

The dome of the Shwedagon Pagoda vaults 300 feet skyward and is covered with 8,688 solid gold slabs. The top is shrouded by a solid gold *seinbu*, which resembles an umbrella and is a mosaic of 5,448 diamonds and 2,317 rubies, with sapphires at its tip. At night, a glow hangs over the city as spotlights send reflected beams of yellowish illumination into the sky. In the shadow of hundreds of smaller spires glowing yellow in the night, I was reminded of the candles on the birthday cake I wasn't having.

After a few days, I was really beginning to like my Pazundaung neighborhood. In 1937, RKO Radio Pictures produced a now forgotten film entitled *You Can't Buy Luck*. Apparently, the producers had not been to Rangoon. A few blocks away, merchants near the Sule Pagoda peddle good fortune in the shadow of this Buddhist shrine. For 100 kyats, bird catchers will let you release a sparrow into the Myanmar skies to ensure your future good fortune.

Instead of blowing out candles on a cake, I forked over my kyats and set a sparrow free. On reflection later, I figured that, for all I knew, my teeny birthday birdie circled around the pagoda once and then flew right back into its cage, awaiting another freedom flight for 100 kyats.

Near the Three Seasons along the waterfront is the majestic

hotel known worldwide as the Strand. It is part of the lineage of great hotels in Southeast Asia built during the heyday of Pax Britannica, like the Oriental Hotel on the Chao Phraya River in Bangkok and the Imperial Hotel in Delhi. With one click of its huge mahogany and glass doors, the Strand Hotel spectacularly, immediately, and intoxicatingly separated me from the din of Rangoon.

While I strolled through the lobby to the bar, I heard Sade whispering her lyrics over the PA. Black lacquer fan blades with gold accents mounted on vaulted ceilings moved the air with silent consistency. I strode across the lobby and followed the arrows pointing me toward the bar.

I found a small round cocktail table and sat down. Immediately my "captain" came over. All afternoon, as I requested, he kept bringing me gin and tonics. I bought a newspaper to see what the rest of the world had been doing. The air-conditioning was blessedly to die for, and the marble floors were clean enough to eat off of.

Across from me a gentlemen with a French accent spoke of business with an Englishwoman. They passed what might have been important papers back and forth while k.d. lang crooned. There were orchids everywhere. It was a perfect, hazy, gin-inspired afternoon.

Exquisite moments are, by definition, fleeting. Happiness. Length.

When I returned to the Three Seasons, I asked Mimi Bo for some help in making arrangements to get north to the ancient Theravada Buddhist center of Old Bagan.

"Yes sir, Mr. Guy," Mimo Bo replied warmly. "I know an agency. I will call."

Soon enough, Min Zaw from the New Place Travels & Tours Co. Ltd. presented his card to me. My brain skipped back to Kay Kay and her New Place Travels sign. I realized I might just be meeting all of her business partners, relatives, or family. I was good with it, mind you. I just find it entertaining how the developing world operates as a fascinating study in how an entire journey can be influenced by one chance meeting, like the one between Kay Kay and me.

Min Zaw's card also had "Zaw Zaw" in parentheses above "Tour Operator." I knew very little about Burmese culture, but I was learning. I knew that the word *Min* used in a boy's name is an aristocratic title such as *King*. The word *Zaw* implies preeminence. I was in pretty good hands, according to his calling card anyway.

Min Zaw was in his twenties, spoke great English, and was full of ideas. He wanted to get me to the Inlay Lake Region. And Kyaiktiyo Pagoda. And then Mandalay. And then Old Bagan. And then ... *Stop!* I thought to myself.

"Min Zaw," I spoke slowly, "I really want to spend some time in Old Bagan. A week, perhaps two." Min Zaw seemed confused that I wasn't looking to cover five tourist sites in three days.

"I think you have organized a lot of tours for a lot of people," I suggested, complimenting him on his checklist of places to go. "But I don't want to rush around Myanmar. I kind of like to find a place and settle in. Can you help me do that?"

"Let's have tea!" he said. In the course of an hour, we finally had a plan. Old Bagan. Air transport. A small place to stay by the Ayeyarwaddy River. Min Zaw would book air tickets and call ahead for reservations so I would have a quiet place to stay.

"Thank you, Mr. Guy Alan!" Min Zaw said, happy that he had the job. "I will make all, and then I will return with your record and we will arrange for payment."

"A pleasure!" I said, extending my hand. "See you again soon."

Later that same day, I asked Mimi Bo for a recommendation for dinner.

"One moment, please. I will ask my aunt," she said, before skipping off into the back office. In a few minutes, she returned with a name scribbled on a piece of paper that I later learned read "Pa Dew Kyew" Chinese Restaurant. This was probably Mimi Bo's aunt's sister's place.

"Lovely!" I said. "I eat Chinese. But how shall I get there?"

"I arrange trishaw for you," the ever-resourceful Mimi Bo declared. "When you like to go?"

At the appointed time I came downstairs, and sure enough, there was a guy on a bicycle with a seat attached to the right side of the rear wheel. It was a man-powered bicycle with a sidecar. I slid into the seat with some hesitancy, and off he pedaled.

"Fear no more," wrote Shakespeare in one of his well-known poems. Then again, he lived in Stratford-upon-Avon in England, which had considerably less traffic than Rangoon. *Honk!* We were in the middle of the road. *Honk!* Now we were on the left. *Honk!* Now we were on the right. We went wherever the car horns and truck horns suggested for us to be.

The streets were dark and dusty, and the probability of occupying the same space at the same time with a much larger metal object added a flavor of excitement that one has to experience to appreciate fully. For 150 kyats, about 25¢, I had risked my life for some Kung Pao chicken.

Mercifully, we pulled up to the restaurant before the laws of physics had an opportunity to apply themselves to us. From the outside it looked like a house with a big picture window carved into what looked like a cement wall. There were papers stuck to the glass, which led me to believe these were the house specials.

Personally, I find the twenty-five characters of the Burmese alphabet gorgeously symmetrical, each nearly an artistic drawing in and of itself. I also admit that I couldn't tell if I was holding a writing right side up or upside down. That ignorance may be on me, but it did not solve the larger problem of ordering food.

As I pushed open the door, I waved what I thought was goodbye to my tricyclist. I didn't know it until an hour later, but he thought I was signaling for him to stay put. So he did. Even though there was no meter perched on his handlebars, I heard my mother whispering in my ear that good manners meant some extra kyat for his commitment.

The restaurant was clean and quiet. I saw more of those non–Home Depot paint colors adorning the walls, and I gathered the distinct smell of incense. The scent reminded me of the incense my Japanese grandparents used to burn in their home in Hawaii in front of their butsudan, a shrine to our ancestors. Somehow I was both far away and surrounded by the familiar at the same time. This wasn't the first time I recognized that every journey was a different path toward home.

An older lady who apparently spoke no English smiled, and brought some hot tea and a menu with modest translations. These are the actual descriptions as they appeared:

> chicken + sauce
> chicken fuyon
> chicken kilan
> liver + ku sai
> roasted fish tail
> hot + dry eel
> leg stew
> steamed leg
> cold leg
> tricolor duck web

No Kung Pao chicken.

I couldn't manage asking what the leg was all about regardless of its varied preparations. Liver? Uh, no thanks. The tricolor duck web sounded wonderfully psychedelic but not so delicious. I went for the no. 1 plus rice. After my meal and a little more tea, I was soon crawling back into the trishaw, which had been waiting the entire time outside to take me back.

The next day, I left the Three Seasons Hotel at 4:30 a.m. for the airport, sadly without seeing the pretty Mimi Bo. It was so early that my taxi careened through nearly empty streets. As we pulled curbside at a nondescript building housing the domestic air terminal in Rangoon, our headlights exposed a mob of people.

There were lots of men in uniform. Some carried guns. Others just milled about in no apparent order. It was a mass of people pushing and shoving and shouting words of a language that was strange to me. Somewhere on the other side of this domestic disturbance was my airplane waiting to take me to the distant northern frontier.

I threaded my way through a crowd that made me feel as if I had been thrown into the middle of a train station, a car wreck, and military exercises all at once. At the very least, the people inside were standing in lines. I immediately secured a place in a column that snaked toward a counter with an Air Mandalay – The Golden Flight sign posted over it.

I soon realized I was not going anywhere fast as there was a queue of equal or greater length for Security. Then there was a check at Immigration. And Customs. And X-ray. And then Post X-ray. And finally came a personal pat down. I expected to have another birthday just getting to the gate.

It took Buddhist-intensity patience to navigate through this unorganized throng of people and these multiple checkpoints. When I completed the maze, I searched for a place to sit. I estimated the boarding area had enough seats for half the number of passengers drifting around.

In the relentless pandemonium, my eyes bounced around. In the span of a minute I saw a cart full of Adidas bags. I watched a toosmall man push a too-big trolley overloaded with luggage. Several monks slept upright, having draped part of their robes over their bald heads. Did that girl's T-shirt read, "Rescue Dog"?

Crates of vegetables were lugged by a series of sweaty men. Someone humped golf clubs. Someone carried a child's tricycle. An Igloo Playmate shot by. Then car parts. And then there were the soldiers patrolling with their AK-47 automatic assault rifles. It was 5:30 a.m. and it was way too early for this shit.

I stood for a while. Then the luck I had bought at the Sule Pagoda paid off. Someone left his seat on a dingy gray bench. Granted, this wasn't the kind of luck that was going to change my life. I was, however, happily off of my feet.

As my eyes wandered about, I spotted a small flight board in the distance. I read the brief list of pending departures, and then I read it a second time. I was particularly concerned that my flight was not listed. In fact, the name of my airline wasn't posted anywhere. I read "Yangon Airways" and "Myanmar Airways," but no "Air Mandalay."

When you are in a foreign country, especially when you don't understand the language, you doubt yourself in ways you would never do at home. As anxiety began to show its dreadful face, I asked myself, *Are any of these announcements saying my flight is canceled?* In exchange for an answer, I gave up my lucky seat.

"Excuse me, but I don't see my flight listed on that board over there!" I said to an unarmed, official-looking guy in uniform. I will never forget as his head swiveled on a pivot like a scene from one of the iconic gunfights photographed in slo-mo by Sam Peckinpah in *The Wild Bunch*. He peered in the direction of my finger.

"But sir," he offered in explanation in the sincerest tone of voice you have ever heard, "it is a small board!"

Indisputably, that it was.

A short time later, an even younger man in uniform walked by carrying a little placard with two tiny brass bells attached to the lower right- and left-hand corners. The board he carried had a flight name and number written on it. As he wound through the throng, he repeated what was inscribed as if he were strolling through the lobby of the Strand Hotel. This impeccably dressed young man was the public address system.

"Four-oh-one, four-oh-one, four-oh-one," he announced with the kind of tone and repetition in his voice that made it sound more like a Buddhist mantra. The bells clinked like champagne glasses at a dinner party.

"Eight-oh-seven, eight-oh-seven, eight-oh-seven," he announced later. And always a delicate "clink, clink, clink" could be heard in the background.

Eventually, the bells tolled for me. "Four-fifty-one" chimed throughout the waiting area. I rose and followed a line of people being escorted across the tarmac to our plane. It was barely capable of holding fifty people, and even I at my modest 5'6" had to tuck my head under the doorway of our twin turboprop airplane.

I plopped into my seat just as the hatch closed with a dull thud. The engines coughed soot until the propellers finally kicked into a spinning blur. I had dreamed of Rangoon and now, miraculously, I'd spent my birthday there. I was already beginning another revolution around Helios and wondered what other adventures were ahead of me in the next 364 days.

I didn't have to wait long. The second we started to taxi for take-off, it occurred to me: *Does Myanmar require regular maintenance of its airplanes or only after one of them falls out of the sky?* You can credit the air maintenance crews or my Sule Pagoda birthday luck. Either way, we were still airborne an hour and a half later.

OLD BAGAN: PRAYERS AND PAGODAS

As we banked slightly left on our landing approach to Nyaung-U Airport, below us were thousands of golden domes and spires of Buddhist temples, pagodas, stupas, monasteries, and religious monuments. They stretched from the Chin Hills to the west, and to what appeared to be the eastern end of the earth.

The Chinese coin dangling from a string around my neck symbolized the vision stretched out before me. The sentimental among us wish to ascribe to the poetic if not entirely factual belief that the square, cutout center of the coin exemplified the four corners of the earth and that the raised, circular rim signified the heavens. Unlike coins of the US realm, which pay tribute to presidents, Native Americans, and at one time, bison, the currency of the Chinese proclaimed with profound romance that its royalty ruled over heaven and earth.

Bagan was once the capital of the First Burmese Empire a thousand years ago. It was so resplendent that the invading army of Emperor Kublai Khan trudged through nearly thirteen thousand

Buddhist structures perched along the banks of the Ayeyarwaddy River. You can picture the soldiers' faces as they gaped at the splendorous result of three centuries of religious construction.

The nearly three thousand structures that remain standing only whisper what the image of four times that number must have looked like. The bricks of ten thousand structures were used in a futile effort to build a protective wall around Old Bagan. The remnants of the walled city still bear the desperation of the Burmese defenders as they exchanged their lives with the Mongol marauders for the vanity of politics and the desire for gold.

The stairway dropped from under the plane with a thud. One by one, I and my fellow passengers exited, trying not to fall flat on our faces onto the tarmac. I grabbed my backpack and walked toward a small airport. Once out the front door, I headed toward to the car park to look for a taxi. Only then did I realize how blazingly hot it was.

After a short ride, I was dropped at the Bagan Thande Hotel, which has historical distinction. Members of the British monarchy once slept here. In 1922, HRH the Prince of Wales, who was later crowned King Edward VIII, came to visit what was then colonial Burma. For this occasion, the government built a two-story wooden structure near the riverbank. I was now living in it.

For about 18 FECs a night, my second-floor suite included a traditional breakfast of *mohinga*, a fish broth over rice noodles, or *kyazanhinga*, a curry broth over steamed rice with fresh coriander and onions. I found the smooth, cool creaky floorboards soothing to my feet and enchanting to my ears.

On many nights, I sat drinking a Tiger Beer in candlelight with my journal in my lap while listening to the birds. The view of the nearby Ayeyarwaddy River was made even more stunning as the sun set in the west and the stars rose. I learned later that I had chosen the cheapest room in the lodge. Price and value are not always related.

I felt like I was living in a tree house. While sitting on my veranda in bare feet and my longyi, I thumbed through a copy of *The Birds of Burma* that had been left on the end table and recited the names of some of my neighbors: the red-wattled lapwing, the Eurasian tree sparrow, the vinous-breasted starling, the green imperial pigeon, the hoopoe, and of course the Burmese shrike. I liked the fact that Old Bagan went to sleep and woke up like I did—slowly.

Before there was enough light to see the thousands of spires piercing the leafy htanaung acacia umbrella, there was a night sky beset with stars, the same ones whose constellations encouraged King Anawratha in the year 1000 CE to initiate a plan of religious building that would last for three hundred years. While the Normans were relishing their conquest of England in 1044, the First Burmese Empire was turning Buddhist. By the end of the fourteenth century, so resplendent was Old Bagan that it was crowned the City of Four Million Pagodas.

In the predawn hours, as the sun struggled to wake itself, temple walls glowed faintly pink, only to turn ever more the color of brick as the morning light began to morph from muted yellow to crisp white. A fragile fog hung between trees in long transparent rows like daily vanishing ridgelines. Drops of water on the tips of east-facing leaves reflected the tint of papaya from morning light that had not yet found its stark blue-white heat. The dry searing temperature of the midday sun was sluggishly on its way.

Buddhist monks and nuns of Old Bagan shuffled in harmony with the great invisible ballet of the movement of the planets around the sun. Buddhists here prayed while walking clockwise around sanctified structures. The act of kora unified the mind in meditation, the body in motion, and the spirit in prayer. Their movement clockwise in synchronicity with the planets of the universe revealed that they knew time, not space, is the road we travel.

It would be impossible to reconcile how Buddhists understood the path of the planets five hundred years before Galileo was convicted of heresy. I had spent some time in Bologna just because of Galileo Galilei, astronomer, physicist, mathematician, and philosopher—among other talents he possessed. In the seventeenth century, Galileo was denied the chair of the department of mathematics at the University of Bologna, Italy, because, of all things, he was too smart. The sun, not the earth, was the center of the universe, Galileo wrote. The Vatican disagreed and declared that Galileo was a real pain in the pope's astronomy.

The Burmese have worked out a balance between reverence and need. You can't, after all, live on the words of prayers alone. Thus, constrained by thousands of scattered ruins and collapsing foundations of Old Bagan's Buddhist structures, fields planted with cabbage, beans, carrots, and other vegetables take on the haphazard shapes of trapezoids, irregular triangles, and other oddly shaped polygons. Cattle dung and goat droppings attest to the meanderings of farm animals between the stupas and temples and decaying monasteries. A falling sun casts long shadows that stretch across the soil and dance between stalwart domes and spires at day's end. The long silhouettes stretch out like the fingers of their Buddha to bless those who toil under the merciless heat of the day.

During the months of winter drought, the temperature rises with the height of the sun. By midday, the heat is strong enough to beat the perception out of you. In open fields and in thickets, unmarked dirt paths cross each other randomly. It was a Buddhist lesson: choose wisely, as the path you take may not lead you to where you wish to go.

I had asked one of the people at the front desk for help in finding a guide to take me around. The following morning I had a note to meet Win Zaw at breakfast. Without any introduction, he walked up to me and handed me his card, which read as follows:

WIN ZAW, BA (History)
Licensed Tour Guide (English)
No. 6 Quarter, Tet Thein Ward
Nyaung Oo (Bagan)
Myanmar.

I've never been a stickler for licensure credentials. In the developing world, they are meaningless, as there are rarely authorities monitoring such things. In a country as unregulated as Myanmar, anyone who can print a card can be what the card says they are. For me it was enough to meet someone local and to trust my intuition regarding his character.

When you are a solitary traveler, this is what you constantly do. The voice inside your head is the only one you trust whether you are in Palankaraya, Borneo, or Lomé, Togo, or Islamabad, Pakistan. The instinct to make the right choice is what keeps you from being robbed, beaten, or worse. It is as simple as that.

The moment I met Win Zaw, I liked him. He was corpulent, was quick to smile, spoke English well, and was greeted warmly by the staff at the lodge. He laughed a lot, which was always a good sign. I told Win Zaw I was going to be in Old Bagan for a while and that I wanted to get into the countryside if possible.

Win Zaw suggested we depart later that week for some of the nearby villages to the south, but he said we needed a car. I offered to rent one. I suspected the place we were about to go belonged to one of his relatives. But a car was a car.

Soon, I was holding another card. This one read as follows:

RENT, A CAR! [*sic*]
MAUNG MYO B.Econ (Economics)
No. 1 Quarter, Tharyarwaddy Ward
Nyaung Oo (Bagan)
Myanmar.

Either Win Zaw and Maung Myo were related to each other or they and the person who had made their cards were related. More important than finding the answer to this question, though, was that I now had a guide and a driver.

We decided to head out the next morning and see what we might find together. Maung Myo drove an old Toyota, Win Zaw gave directions from the backseat, and I rode shotgun. We drove past goatherds and maize farmers. Women balanced water pots on their heads as they walked along dirt roads. Others squatted while smoking homemade cheroots. As we drove farther away from Bagan, villages slipped away and the tilled fields of farmers yielded to what little development there was surrounding my hotel.

"What's that?" I blurted out, pointing to a dilapidated walled area.

Win Zaw checked the map. Nothing.

I checked the map. Nothing.

Maung Myo checked the map. Nothing.

That meant we had to stop.

After some effort, we agreed that this must be Tsu Taung Pyi Monastery. Neither Win Zaw nor Maung Myo had ever been inside, so that was a good enough reason for us to enter. The place was in terrible shape, with collapsed walls that once protected the temple. Now, it was a shell—and barely that. I walked around a third corner with Win Zaw and Maung Myo behind me, where we came across a lone woman in deep meditation. She never moved. Not a flinch. Not a breath. Not a peek to see who we were.

"It is a wonderful concentration, yes?" whispered Win Zaw.

Here in this room with sun-bleached blue walls was this solitary figure consumed by the emptiness of her mind in an equally empty place. She was in a different world.

Win Zaw and I moved around her in opposite directions so as to not cross in front of her. As I looked behind her, I saw pink fabric hanging from a tree and realized that she, with her shaved head, was one of the tens of thousands of pink nuns of Myanmar. The nuns, who wear pink to honor Buddha, renounce all worldly possessions.

Win Zaw met a second, much younger nun who explained that she and the matriarch in meditation lived there without water or electricity. The last monk had died some time ago; they were the only nuns left in the monastery. Like all of the monks and nuns, they lived on the benevolence of others. I became one of the benevolent by leaving some kyats near a flower vase. Then I waved to Win Zaw and Maung Myo, indicating that it was time to go.

We returned to my royal residence late in the afternoon, where we discussed the next day's events over tea and snacks. Win Zaw set a route to some of the villages on the outskirts of Old Bagan.

"Maybe we stop and have a walk in some of the villages?" Win Zaw proposed.

"Perfect!" I exclaimed with excitement.

"Sir, you must be understanding me now!" Win Zaw then pleaded.

"Okay, Win Zaw, " I said, "I am understanding you."

"Sir," Win Zaw continued, "you must promise me you will not eat in the villages. The water, sir, is no good. It will hurt your stomach."

I was touched by his concern that I not contract what clearly was a veiled reference to traveler's diarrhea.

"Yes! Win Zaw," I said, trying to assuage his fear, "on my mother's eyes, I promise, no food or water."

The following morning, we all met for tea and breakfast before pushing off. As we left Old Bagan, Win Zaw suggested we stop and visit Ananda Temple, a masterpiece of Mon architecture built in the twelfth century.

Some things never lose their majesty. The main hall left me gawking like I'd done the first time I walked into the Duomo Cathedral in Milan. I wrote that the Duomo began its marble construction in the 1300s and had taken what can only be described as "cathedral time," nearly seven hundred years, to complete. Ananda Temple was that kind of stupefying moment.

While wandering around the grounds, I met U Nareinda, a monk visiting from Thein Daung Monastery.

"Minga lau bah!" I said, beaming.

"Hello!" my robed friend offered in good English. I always felt a tad unbalanced talking to someone draped in fabric the color of burnt sienna. It was not U Nareinda's fault, for sure. It was just that so much seemed to separate me from him. He had nothing beyond his begging bowl and robes, yet he displayed the kind of joy one would have if the world were his oyster.

Unlike U Nareinda, I lived secure in the knowledge that I had the comfort of the Bagan Thande Hotel to go home to and that I could count on a shower, clean clothes, and a meal at the beginning and end of each day. These monks and the pink nuns I met the day before have none of this security in food or shelter. Yet there is calm and peace within them. Maybe in my next life.

U Nareinda had been a monk since he was twenty-three years old. That was four decades ago. Born to a Christian father and a Buddhist mother, he entered the monastery and never left. It gave him a perspective that expressed itself in surprising ways.

"If you see a good sunset," he proclaimed as if something grand was about to follow, "you remember your lover; if you eat good food, you remember your mother!" U Nareinda then burst out laughing.

I thought it was pretty funny myself, especially coming from a monk. So did Win Zaw and Maung Myo. After walking through the grounds and talking for a while, I told U Nareinda we had to go, but I left a donation for the temple. I'm not even sure why he went to all the trouble, but he completed some kind of form documenting my donation. I still have that certificate. It reminds me of U Nareinda and the lesson he shared about living a life that has *value*. Enjoy each day; that's all there is.

The three of us piled back into Maung Myo's car, and again we were off. After we arrived at Moenhatkone, Win Zaw and I ditched Maung Myo, leaving him with the car. We walked along a trail that was the dried creek bed of the stream that ran through the center of the village during the rainy season. Life here seemed like life in the country as it existed most anywhere in Southeast Asia. Women transported exaggerated loads of wood, vegetables, and rice balanced upon their heads, necks, or backs. Other women stood and threshed harvested grain from the stems as the wind suspended the chaff in the air.

Men on bullock carts dragged heavy barrels of water from the central well to thatch-roofed homes. The nearest freshwater well was over five kilometers away. Young boys and girls rode their bicycles in play. Women and young ladies strolled about in batik cloth the colors of which could only have been created by a Crayola scientist gone mad. This was what a painting might have looked like if Paul Gauguin had shipped off to Burma instead of Tahiti.

Maung Myo met us on the other side of the village. Soon we were in a tiny place called Ganga. According to Win Zaw, it wasn't on the map either. We got out again and left Maung Myo with a promise to return in less than an hour.

Ganga was a quiet village right up to the point when we heard a woman shriek. The parched air was filled with dust, birdcalls, and barking dogs. Win Zaw and I ran over toward the commotion. Several men stood over a pile of thatch being used to replace a roof. They beat the pile repeatedly with wooden poles until a viper slithered out.

Barefoot villagers scattered in every direction. A nearby woman grabbed one of the petrified kids and ran. A man clubbed the viper several times before lifting the lifeless body draped over his stick. With that assurance, everyone within eyeshot knew it was safe. Win Zaw and I departed happy, knowing that all had ended well except for the snake.

With the setting sun on the horizon, we decided to head back to cold Tiger Beers on my veranda, to watch as the Ayeyarwaddy River shimmered, and to relax in our viper-free zone. As a special treat, I ordered Mandalay Rum over ice with a lime to celebrate yet another day that was not my birthday.

Days passed. Nights were cool as the winter winds forced me to wear my fleece to keep warm in the chilled air blowing down from the northern mountains in Bangladesh and China. I walked dusty paths early in the morning, sometimes with Win Zaw sometimes not. I was wandering again.

Soon enough I was back in Rangoon making arrangements with

Min Zaw to get to Bangkok. Having arrived without reservations, I was disheartened to find out that the Three Seasons Hotel was booked. Mimi Bo, however, sent me just four blocks away to the Haven Inn. It was a family-operated rooming house, which I assumed was the property of another one of Mimi Bo's aunts.

After paying for my room, I asked to take a hot shower. Three of them, the patriarch and two women, spoke among themselves with the seriousness of Catholic cardinals holding a conclave to elect a new pope. After a short time, the younger lady left the room and then soon returned to hand me a note that read as follows:

FOR HOT WATER
1. SWIFT [*sic*] ON HOT WATER TAP
2. WAIT FOR SIX MINIUTES [*sic*]
HAVEN INN

All of a sudden I wanted to give the Three Seasons Hotel another season. But the Haven Inn was clean and quiet, and at US$10, it was a modest home sweet home. I only needed a room for one night, as my departure had been set for the following morning.

It took me a while to embrace the idea that Rangoon had been a recurrent daydream for me throughout my youth and now that dream had become a reality. With age, I learned sometimes you have to be awake to experience your best dreams. And here, it seemed, I suddenly was.

The day I departed from Nyaung-U Airport, I glanced back one last time as my Golden Flight rose above the City of Four Million Pagodas. I considered how much I treasured my birthday tradition.

Granted, it's not for everyone. Spending a birthday alone is an acquired taste. But as U Nareinda's life represented, there are few gifts more precious than living a day exceptionally well, whether it's your birthday or just another Wednesday.

STONED, COLD, AND HUNGRY
IN THE KARAKORAM

It was the summer of 2004 and the temperature was −25°C at night.

I was camped in the western Himalayan Mountains of northern Pakistan at the foot of K2 on assignment to cover the fiftieth anniversary of the first successful ascent. For that reason alone, base camp was especially active, as no fewer than eleven expeditions from around the world had come to climb and watch the Italians repeat history. I was the one-man Hawaiian expedition.

In 1953, Sir Edmund Hillary of New Zealand and Tenzin Norgay climbed Mt. Everest, the world's tallest mountain at 29,029 feet. The following year, the race was on for K2's summit at 28,251 feet. On July 31, 1954, K2 surrendered to an Italian expedition led by world-famous geologist and adventurer Ardito Desio, who famously recounts planting his country's flag in *La Conquista del K2.*

In the Karakoram Range, within which K2 sits, being high is relative. At nearly 18,000 feet, my tent was higher than the highest permanent settlement in the world by more than half a mile. The good people of La Rinconada in Peru lived at an altitude claimed to be the maximum height of human habitability. I got your maximum height.

The difference between these two stone and ice behemoths is more than 778 vertical feet. Consider that the Everest Base Camp is accessible by climbing for seven or eight days. K2 Base Camp takes nearly twice as long to reach, making it the most remote base camp of any major mountain anywhere. This inaccessibility causes critical supply problems for food, fuel, and equipment.

Failed attempts at K2's summit are no disgrace. Many have tried, and very few have succeeded. In the last sixty years, only 306 climbers have summited K2, while nearly 6,000 have summited Mt. Everest. Perhaps that explains why the Baltistanis call their mountain Chogori, "King of Mountains."

Experienced Western climbers call K2 "the Killer Mountain," citing the grim statistic that one out of every four climbers dies making a summit attempt. But everyone doesn't die while climbing along the Abruzzi Ridge or the Magic Line routes of K2. Some just end up dead.

Like Tatsuo Harada. This summer, we found his body after he had disappeared nearly a decade ago. He had been entombed alive along with five other Japanese climbers under an avalanche of snow and ice that barreled over him while he lay sleeping in his tent at base camp, the safest place he could have been on the entire mountain. I imagined Tatsuo warm and dreaming of the cherry blossoms back in Tokyo for which he was departing the next morning. His dream ended that night; he never saw home again.

If that isn't enough death for you, the region within which K2 stands is claimed simultaneously by feuding Pakistan and India and, depending when you ask, China. I read a story once that described Jammu-Kashmir as the "highest battlefield on earth." Clever. It is supreme irony that there are people who believe that hypothermia, altitude sickness, crevasse falls, avalanches, and disorienting fatigue are not enough ways to die. So they add bullets to that list.

Base camp, however, was anything but dour. Even if we all understood that nowhere here was safe, still we laughed. We told stories. Elation was everywhere, swallowing up the cold. It was the poet Jack Gilbert who wrote, "We must risk delight. ... We must have the stubbornness to accept our gladness in the ruthless furnace of this world." K2 gave us the chance to live every bit of that wisdom.

Living at K2's base camp for three months altered the prism

through which I perceived the world. I stopped using the word *white* altogether because it did not begin to describe the subtle shades of snow and ice that surrounded me. How my tent flapped in the night told me whether a bitterly cold wind was blowing from China or a warmer one was coming from Pakistan. I knew it was three hundred freezing steps to the latrine east of my camp and that it would take me ten minutes to dress before I could step outside. Bodily functions, like dinner, were planned ahead of time.

On a clear night, the blackness of the sky unveiled the Milky Way as just one layer of stars layered on top of other layers of stars not visible at lower elevations. I actually heard silence, which sounded like a snowflake as it landed onto the Godwin-Austen Glacier. I knew how far away an avalanche had fallen from the guttural rumbling it made as it yielded to gravity. I had left the planet I knew for a mysterious one.

Climbing season ends in August, at which time, for most teams, it was a race back down to Askoli and then Skardu farther below. I made my way back with my Baltistani guide, Rozi. As we wound downward, we stopped at various camps scattered along the Baltoro Glacier for food and to rest. One camp called Sansanchu was near the Dumordo River.

I remember that camp distinctly because of Haji Ali. I recall his face as clear as gin. Haji Ali had only one good eye. His clothes were tattered and soiled. His teeth were stained red from chewing *pan-tamul*, a mild intoxicant extracted from the betel nut.

"As-salaam alaikum!" he grunted in the yellow light.

As Haji Ali stood in the corner, I took the dirty brass pipe handed to me, sucked on the mouthpiece, and watched as the olive-brown chip glowed brightly and the pungent smell of hashish filled the tent. I considered the idea that possession means hard time in Islamabad. But not in this tent at Camp Sansanchu. Not in the Karakoram Mountains of Pakistan along the banks of the Dumordo River. At nearly three miles above sea level, literally and figuratively, I was above the law.

Outside may have been brutally cold, but inside I embraced the effects of tetrahydrocannabinol, the wizard behind the curtain that allowed me to move marijuana off the list of illegal substances and into the realm of naturopathic medicines. After I took that first long, deep drag, my aching legs became comfortably limp for the first time in three months. My feet stopped pulsing where blisters had burst and raw spots throbbed. I didn't feel the cuts and bruises on my hands. Pain faded away with each puff of smoke. Suddenly, I was good.

By the time I reached the banks of the Dumordo River, I'd been coming down for days. My rescue-yellow North Face VE25 tent had been home for over two months. Daily temperatures on the Godwin-Austen Glacier hovered at around shiver. But when night came, it was colder than the heart of the last person who broke up with you.

I hadn't been to Afghanistan, but I thanked the Pashtun tribes just in case they had grown the cannabis somewhere within their mysterious tribal borders. I had no idea how hashish was transported to this tent, but long live the Pashtuns if they helped.

Seeing a mountain range once a part of Genghis Khan's empire was thrilling in and of itself. To help you appreciate fully this region and its influence on our lives today, the importance of Jack Weatherford's notable achievement with his *New York Times* best-selling book *Genghis Khan and the Making of the Modern World* can't be understated. Even absent knowledge of its history, climbing in the Karakoram was so exhilarating that it has seduced an abundance of climbers to come here for nearly a century. There seemed to be no end to the adventurers eager to wager their lives against something as intangible as bragging rights.

Most mountaineers didn't do it for the fame. Mountaineering was an exclusive club. Nonmembers knew little to nothing about mountains, climbing gear, or the people who were its OCD aficionados. You either were a climber or you weren't.

Haji Ali threw back the door flap of the cook tent and stepped to the nearest corner. Six Baltistani porters, Rozi Ali, and I sat around a tiny kerosene stove brewing green tea and watching as a few cardamom seeds floated just beneath the surface.

Not so far away, the Dumordo River churned like my gurgling bowels. Getting sick was part of living here. Everyone got sick sooner or later with the gut-wrenching, knife-stabbing, shit-in-your-pants kind of runs. Now, it was my turn. Again.

My intestines repeatedly expelled an infectious organism from inside of me by wringing my lower alimentary canal into knots with such convulsive force that Western physicians have given it an artful, almost elegant name: explosive diarrhea. That sums it up pretty much.

The Dumordo River was doing the same thing to the earth. It was violently discharging an icy runoff so opaque with effluvium that it looked more like liquid concrete than water.

The summer ice melt had swollen the waters of the Dumordo that streaked passed Camp Sansanchu. I liked that name. In Balti it means "clean water." Romantic. Untrue. But romantic.

This season, the river proved itself to be as ruthless as the mountain by drowning three porters in one day. Sick of trudging fifty pounds for six hours for about US$5 a day, three porters took a shortcut and tried to ford Dumordo at a narrow section. Rather than trekking a four-mile detour that led to a rickety wooden bridge, they ended up downstream and dead.

Unlike them, Rozi Ali and I made camp freezing cold and hungry. The icy night air raged down from China and drove Rozi Ali and me into the comparative warmth of Sansanchu's cook tent. When I threw back the tent flap, I saw a half dozen weather-beaten, sunburned men sitting in a circle on a blue tarp. As mountain customs demanded, they acknowledged Rozi and me and then invited us to sit.

The light from the kerosene lantern cast a glow on their stingy smiles that gave them yellow dogs' teeth. The canvas of the tent slapped sporadically as the wind whipped up the narrow channel cut by the river. I sat down between two men who silently parted to make room for me around the food plates.

I reached across one man, tore off a piece of roti, dipped it into cold goat meat curry, and then rammed it into my mouth. I ignored the dirt under my fingernails and the dust on my shirt and pants. The mud that stuck to my boots was mud that stuck to my boots. No one noticed.

Over the summer, I had become accustomed to eating with strangers. I reached into the center of the circle and dipped another piece of unleavened bread into the bowl. I was at ease sharing dal or yak stew. In my cook tent, I had hosted many strangers who came, ate, and sometimes slept, leaving the following morning. Some were friends of Rozi Ali, my cook. Some were friends of Rozi Ali's friends.

In the Karakoram, no one ever gets turned away when seeking food or shelter. Ever. One day, sooner or later, you know it will be you standing at a tent flap cold and hungry. Today was our day.

When Alexander the Great marched his Greek army across this region on his way to the China Sea, he learned a tribal lesson: "A friend of a friend is my friend; a friend of my enemy is my enemy." The British died by the tens of thousands at the Khyber Pass learning that lesson. The Soviets in Afghanistan learned it a century later. It may go without saying, but it is better to have friends in this part of the world.

The Karakoram taught me other lessons; for example, the absence of most everything brings clarity. Take stew. The meat in the stew, if there was meat, oftentimes was goat. Infrequently, it was yak. In either case, it was almost always gristle. You chewed it, and it chewed back.

When you are hungry, food is food. It is the privilege of the rich to choose, because they can afford to buy choices. Here, the choice was to eat bad food or go hungry. Clarity.

The surprising corollary to that rule was that the absence of almost everything results in charity. In the presence of nearly nothing, we all shared what little we had. Sometimes it was everything we had—the last of the tea and lentils, all of the roti and stew.

Even in the sparse world of the Karakoram, no one complained that there was never enough to eat. There never was. But living like a tribe meant you accepted that whatever there was would go around. Gluttony lived down in the cities. Up here, at the end of the night, everyone went to sleep a little bit hungry.

I stared at Haji Ali's one good eye as his head darted and jerked unnaturally, struggling to see. Having been left with one eye to do the work of two, he had a desperate look on his face as his head shifted and tilted in odd directions to provide his one good eye with a full field of vision.

Haji Ali's vacant eye looked like the eye of a marble bust in a museum. His milky-white right eye glared ahead uselessly.

Haji Ali's *pakol*, which sat cockeyed on his head, was the traditional style of the Afghans and Pashtuns who lived in the northwestern valleys of Pakistan's frontier provinces. His cream-colored hat was soiled badly, much like the knee-length shirt of his *shalwar kameez*. His tattered pakol and the absence of his two front teeth made his chocolate-tanned face appear even darker and more sinister than it might actually have been. Haji Ali was, by any measure, ugly.

The Baltistani porters I had traveled with during these past months along the Baltoro Glacier basin were doing what the men of the Hunza Valley of Pakistan did for work. For nearly one hundred years, foreigners came here and trekked fifteen or twenty days, one way, to reach the base of K2. They paid the porters in cash. After four months of backbreaking work, hauling food and supplies more than sixteen thousand feet up the mountain, the porters earn enough money to live the remaining months lazily until the next climbing season.

But foreigners always remained foreign to them. The porters carried their goods. They cooked for them. They even sang their traditional songs. Few foreigners, however, chose to engage them beyond that menial but necessary service. I doubt most Westerners could even locate where Baltistan was on a map.

Muslim historians refer to Baltistan as Little Tibet and to Ladakh as Great Tibet. This is also the region of the mythical earthly paradise of Shangri-la that is spoken of in the novel *Lost Horizons*.

The cook tents were where the Baltistanis ate and slept, and visited with their kinsmen. Streams of porters passed through camps just like this one at Sansanchu. The camps were scattered up and down the valley as welcome respites from hauling goods and gear to and from K2. The Baltistanis served chai to anyone, kinsman or not, who would sit, drink green tea, and share the news that somehow emerged from Askoli or Skardu far below.

Every breath Haji Ali took formed a tiny puffy cloud emerging from his mouth and disappearing in the warmth of our tent. A few looked up. I watched them as their eyes met Haji Ali's one good eye just long enough to acknowledge each other. Most returned to eating or smoking or conversing in Urdu, Pashto, Kashmiri, or any other of the dozen or so languages of the region.

A couple of weeks before, I had seen that haunting empty gaze of Haji Ali's useless right eye. It belonged to a distant cousin of the American bison. A yak had been driven to one of the cook tents at base camp belonging to an Italian expedition.

In Pakistan, meat is dead weight. When you want beef or goat, it comes to you on the hoof—self-propelled.

After the yak arrived to the excitement of the entire camp, I watched as several porters slowly surrounded the animal. One of the men reached under the beast and tied a rope around its right front leg. The eyes of the animal widened.

While the yak began to push and pull against the men trying to hold it in place, the rope attached to the right front leg was then looped around the two rear legs and pulled taut. In one great heave, the men constricted the rope around the three legs, and by bringing the legs together to a single point, they caused the yak to lose balance and fall onto its side like a felled tree.

"No!" the yak shrieked in that long, nasally, guttural voice that sounds like "moo" to children. Its nostrils flared. Air moved in and out of its lungs as if a steam engine were trapped inside.

The remainder of the men standing around jumped on top of the writhing yak to keep it from working itself free of the rope. Its head bounced uncontrollably on the ground as one eye glared heavenward.

Death is death to all living things. A developed cerebrum and an understanding of Jean-Paul Sartre's *No Exit* isn't a predicate to comprehending *the end*. The very concept of death is not susceptible to rational thought because it is not comprehensible intellectually.

In animals, the abyss arises as instinctual fear. And fear is intuited by both humans and animals. It is a perception of imminent eternal extinction. It is the same intuition that tells an animal it is safe to drink, as well as when it is time to flee.

In this brute animal's eyes, I saw fear. The yak jerked and tussled to set itself free. The men laughed while being bounced in the air with each kick.

"Allahu Akbar!" I heard in the distance from a stout bearded man as he raked the blade of a long knife across a sharpening stone. "God is great!" he recited under his breath with mechanical devotion. In the sun, tiny beads of sweat dropped from his forehead. Every so often he would run his sleeve across the length of his face as he continued his motion.

"Allahu Akbar!" he whispered.

This was halal, the ritual of Islamic slaughter. The butcher was in no hurry in spite of the effort of the men to restrain the thrashing yak. He moved the blade across the stone with the speed of ice melting. He never lifted his eyes as his hand moved from the darkness of his own shadow into the gleaming sunlight.

"Allahu Akbar!" he repeated.

Periodically he would flip the blade from one side to the other. The work of the stone and of the muscles that drove the instrument back and forth became apparent as the cutting edge shone like a bright white line.

The butcher again held the knife up to his eyes for inspection. Then, with the pressure of bird's feather, he ran his thumb along the edge to feel its readiness. He turned it over and inspected it like a jeweler with a loupe. Another pass of the thumb. Nodding to himself in satisfaction, he rose to his feet.

"Allahu Akbar!" he announced with his prayer. It was time.

He walked to the yak and knelt behind its head. With his left hand, the butcher pointed to two of the men to pull back on the head of the yak until its pulsating throat was fully exposed. The eye of the yak darted ferociously back and forth like Haji Ali's one good eye. In the next second, the knife sliced across its hairy black neck.

"Allahu Akbar!" the butcher prayed, as he forced the blade deeper and deeper into the quivering flesh. "God is great!"

Blood spurted all over the hands of the butcher and onto the rocks that cradled the yak's head. The beast's legs kicked spastically as the windpipe was totally severed and its lungs lost connection to life-giving air. Its stomach threw up whatever constituted its last meal, and the stench of digestion, urine, feces, and fresh blood wafted passed me.

With each heartbeat, there was more blood. "God is great!" the butcher continued to pray, knife in hand. The impurities within the beast continued to spill onto frozen earth. With each beat of its heart, the yak cleansed itself of its own uncleanness. This was the Islamic way. The tradition of thousands of years was being acted out once again.

All at once, the eye yielded. Lifeless, its fear vanished. The eye froze into an opaque grayish white stone. That was the look of Haji Ali's useless right eye. That was what was so disturbing about his appearance. It was looking at life and death at the same time, when the two may never otherwise coexist.

I watched as Haji Ali smiled slightly. The men ignored his presence. I didn't know then that he wasn't just visiting. He was working.

Haji Ali's job suited him. To the north of Camp Sansanchu was a footbridge. It was, as far as I knew, only one of two bridges along the entire length of the Baltoro basin, which stretched 115 kilometers into the Central Karakoram Range. It was an unavoidable fact that you had to cross Haji Ali's bridge or else die like the three porters who had tried to detour around it. I understood then that his demonic grin arose from a pecuniary joy. He was counting heads and adding rupees.

He had no uniform, no identification of service in an official capacity, and no apparent authority, yet everyone at Camp Sansanchu deferred to him and paid his tax of twenty rupees a person to cross. Allah only knows what he did with the toll. But collect it he did.

"Rozi," I whispered, leaning over to grab a piece of roti and turning to catch his attention. Rozi Ali was not just my personal Baltistani cook. He was also my porter, my guide, and after the last three months together, my friend.

Together, we had navigated the dangerous serac field en route from base camp to the foot of the Abruzzi Ridge on K2 leading to the higher camps. We warned each other of crevasses that stretched so far beneath our feet that we couldn't see bottom. We helped each other dig out from under a couple of huge snowfalls. We had gone on a search and rescue one night after we heard from one of the Spanish expeditions that Rozi Ali's nephew had frozen his hands and feet while making a summit charge.

As the months passed, we laughed, drank green tea, and stared at the stars. We ate, exchanged gifts, and shared stories of our families. We stayed up late in the cook tent night after night holding language classes. The Karakoram had made us allies against the harshness of the summer storms.

Rozi Ali gave me a subtle turn of his head to acknowledge he had heard his name but not enough to call undue attention from the others. I threw both of my eyes at the corner of the tent where Haji Ali was standing. My eyebrows formed a question mark.

"No good man," said Rozi Ali under cover of the laughter from the others. This came from a man who had never spoken ill of anyone until that night. And just that fast, Haji Ali dissolved into the night like the smoke from our hashish pipe. He was there and then he wasn't.

Dead tired and feeling contentedly numbed, Rozi Ali and I begged off with an "Inshallah" (God willing). We would see them all in the morning.

The next morning arrived too early. In fact, Rozi came to my tent so much earlier than usual that it was still black as pitch when he showed up with green tea and roti.

"Member, good sleeping?" he asked with a grin. He called me "member" often, although sometimes he would say "Mr. Guy," depending on his mood. It came out in all shapes and forms.

"Member, hungry?"

"Member, sick?"

"Member, cold?"

"Member want green tea?"

It took some time to get used to being called "member." For Rozi Ali, like many of the Baltistani cooks and porters, it was easier to call a foreigner "member" than trying to recall a name. For me it was particularly funny because I had come to K2 as my own one-man Hawaii expedition, so I was the only member of my team.

"As-salaam alaikum, Rozi," I said, placing my right hand over my heart, somewhat startled by the early call.

"Wa alaikum salaam," he replied, always smiling boyishly. This was our morning ritual. Even as a Buddhist, I shared the blessing of Allah with him first thing.

"Member yesterday eating, putting, walking! I am speaking!" Rozi Ali declared in order to coax me to urgent and immediate action.

"Are we leaving early today, Rozi? Is something wrong?" I asked before I was even fully awake.

Quickly, I sipped some tea, crammed some bread into my mouth, and began to stuff my sleeping pod into my pack along with my cameras and the few other personal belongings I had managed to bring down from my glacial home. The avalanches that fell regularly by day and night above, and sometimes through base camp, taught me to sleep lightly, wake quickly, and move at a moment's notice.

"Yesterday, Mr. Guy," Rozi Ali said. "Haji Ali no good man!"

In spite of all my lessons, I could never get Rozi Ali to understand the difference between the concepts of yesterday, today, and tomorrow. To him, everything happened yesterday, regardless of when it really happened or when it was going to happen.

"Okay, Rozi," I said, not grasping the urgency to eat, pack, and leave. It was enough for me to know that we were leaving now and that it had something to do with Haji Ali not being a good man.

In less than fifteen minutes, we had *yesterday eating, putting, and walking*, as Rozi Ali had urged. We made our way by flashlight as we passed the camp markers at Camp Sansanchu. Once on the trail toward the bridge over the Dumordo River, Rozi Ali started laughing.

"Why laughing, Rozi?" I asked, his contagious grin beginning to creep onto my face.

"I am speaking," began Rozi Ali, as if he needed to announce he was talking.

"Haji Ali no good man. Haji no making. Member Rozi, no making!" And then he began laughing really hard.

Rozi Ali was walking fast even though he was carrying just this side of twenty-five kilos (fifty-five pounds). Among other things, I had my cameras, two hundred rolls of exposed film, four lenses, and a tripod that came to the far side of twenty kilos (forty-four pounds). In other words, we were not traveling light, but we were moving like we were.

"Rozi, good walking!" I said, nearly breathless. I wanted to know why we were moving so damn fast.

"Looking," said Rozi Ali, pointing back at Camp Sansanchu. "Haji bridge police. Coming!" He laughed as we continued to walk way too fast for the weight we were lugging.

"Haji Ali no good, man!" he repeated. "Putting bridge," said Rozi Ali finally, getting to the point while gesturing downward with two fingers above his shirt pocket.

I got it. Rozi Ali wasn't going to pay twenty rupees to a man who was going to pocket the cash. So, for about forty-two cents each, we were in a race to the bridge over the Dumordo River with Haji Ali in hot pursuit after having discovered our premature, unpaid absence. By the time Haji Ali noticed we were not only out of our tent but also off-site, we had a good thirty minutes' head start.

But Haji Ali wasn't carrying a load. And if I could have seen his one good eye, I am certain it would have been filled with determination. Instead, I was worried that our nearly one hundred pounds of gear was going to feel a lot heavier soon.

Rozi Ali knew well enough that I had far more than forty rupees on me. It wasn't the eighty-four cents as much as it was the principle. That explained how we found ourselves in the dark *good walking*, breathing hard, laughing, and pointing behind us like naughty schoolchildren.

"Haji Ali fast walking!" Rozi Ali cried as he glanced back, taunting our pursuer. Haji Ali was no quitter.

"Rozi!" I shouted while panting, "member here!" I caught up to him and showed him forty rupees.

Rozi Ali smiled, turned away, and never broke stride as my legs began to burn. Making it to the bridge over the Dumordo River before Haji Ali caught us became a parable of Greek proportions. It was more than forty miserable rupees. It was a race between right and wrong.

With each step toward the bridge, we were writing our own play. It would conclude as a comedy or tragedy depending on this very footrace.

As we turned the bend and headed due north toward the Chinese border, we could finally see Haji Ali's rickety excuse for a footbridge. Pounded together from scrap boards and driftwood, it was kind even to give it the dignity of calling it a bridge.

Rozi Ali was right. Twenty rupees a person was too much to pay for the privilege of falling to your death into the freezing waters of the Dumordo River. Paying to die was reason enough for Rozi Ali to demand of me to *yesterday eating, putting, and walking* in these early hours.

When we finally reached the threshold of the bridge, Rozi Ali stopped and smiled at the distant and now impotent effort of Haji Ali.

"Picture, Mr. Guy?" asked my smirking Baltistani friend, tilting his head slightly as if to punctuate his inquiry.

"Sure, Rozi, why not?" I said happily as I slung my pack to the ground and reached into the top zippered pouch. It was as if our supreme effort to make right triumph over wrong had earned us all the time in the world. I didn't even bother to look back.

"Okay, Rozi Ali going!" he declared. I watched with suspended breath as Rozi Ali bounced along as the entire length of undulating boards swayed as much left and right as it did up and down. The support wires oscillated with each step. As I stood on solid ground, I realized I had no clue what the tensile strength was for steel cable. Today, over the raging waters of the Dumordo River, it seemed a lot flimsier than the word *steel* sounded.

I questioned whether it would support one person, let alone two people. I chose to wait for Rozi Ali to arrive at the far side before I set off myself.

"Okay, Mr. Guy!" he said, waving energetically and laughing at my apparent hesitation.

"Allahu Akbar!" I shouted to Rozi Ali as I shouldered my pack and began the longest seventy-five-foot trek of my life.

"Khudah haffiz!" I exclaimed in the direction of Haji Ali as I set my feet back onto firm ground. (May God be your guardian!)

Rozi Ali repeated my wish. Then we turned away from the bridge at the Dumordo River, laughing and moving once again toward Askoli village and the green valley surrounding Skardu, far from the icy heavens.

That was the kind of clarity I learned high in the Karakoram.

Hunger. Fear. Charity. Death. Joy. The moment in the morning when I opened my eyes and understood I was still alive. That I had the limitless possibilities of one more day. And time to wonder what everyone else was doing down on earth.

THE ROADS THROUGH DAMASCUS

Today was Ramadan 27, 1428, in Amman.

In another world I knew, it was October 9, 2007. Either way, it was just one more Tuesday night when Horse of God suggested we go to the Christian Quarter to drink whiskey and eat lamb kabobs. Alcohol was banned in the Muslim neighborhood where we were.

I had arrived in Jordan just six days earlier via Qatar and Bangkok. *Arabian Horse Magazine* had accepted my proposal for a story, which oddly enough began with a discussion I'd had at K2 base camp three years earlier.

Karl was a German photographer shooting for *Der Spiegel*. He mentioned to me that a few years earlier he had found a wealthy gentleman in Amman who created an institute that taught the ancient art of Arabian horsemanship. He suggested that it would make an ideal story for one of the US magazines. Three years later I was in Amman.

Mohammed Muhraddin, whose name means "Horse of God," was my best friend in Jordan and, self-admittedly, a marginally practicing Muslim. I read somewhere in the Quran about the prohibitions against drinking and chasing women. That neither enhanced nor diminished our friendship; we simply declared it ignorable dogma.

In Amman, we were like Don Quixote and Sancho Panza, wanderers in the middle of the Middle East seeking others who loved art, music, literature, food, tobacco, alcohol, and the occasional tryst. We tilted at windmills openly in a place not known for its tolerance of free spirits.

I first met Horse of God at a teahouse in the central part of the city. "As-salaam alaikum!" I said with my right hand over my heart and my left hand with open palm pointing toward the empty chair. I invited him to share my table when I noticed that all of the other chairs in the café had been taken.

"Wa alaikum salaam!" Horse of God replied with a big smile. Then he sat down. After he settled in, he stretched across the table and offered me a cigarette.

"Shukran!" I mumbled while holding the cigarette in my lips and lighting it.

Horse of God smiled back. We sat for a while together but remained speechless over the invisible yet enormous chasm created by language. I scribbled notes in my journal. He gazed out over central Amman, smoking and drinking sweet tea. He wore oversized bifocal glasses, a quilted black vest over a long-sleeve plaid shirt, and a black cap that reminded me of the hat worn by John Lennon in *A Hard Day's Night*.

"You ar-r-re Amer-r-rican?" Horse of God asked after a fair length of silence. His English startled me. Before I could answer, he waved his hand in a circle above his head, signaling to the waiter to bring us more tea. His low, raspy voice trilled the *r*'s, which made him sound more European than Persian. I wasn't far off, as Poland soon entered our conversation.

His language skills built a bridge that spanned my halting Arabic so that both of us could finally properly meet. Horse of God had a Pakistani father and an Iraqi mother. Born in Basra, his talent for painting revealed itself when he was a teenager. He was so gifted as an artist that at twenty-two he received a scholarship from the Academy of Fine Arts in Warsaw, Poland. He came to love, in his words, "modern art, Polish vodka, and European women."

His studies and probably some vodka led him to a young woman whose parents were Polish and Hungarian. They fell in love, married, and soon had what Horse of God described as "children of the United Nations." He eventually returned home to Iraq and became one of the dominant stars of the art scene in Baghdad.

"If you left Iraq for Jordan two years ago," I observed, as if I knew what I was talking about, "that was just before all hell broke loose."

"We are not Ir-r-raqi, or Syr-r-rian, or Egyptian," Horse of God proclaimed in his booming voice.

He went off on a tirade.

"Before, we were Babylonian and Assyrian and Persian. We are all humans! Why are we so afraid of each other?" he asked rhetorically.

It was a hell created by our own fears, I acknowledged, raising my shoulders in unison. This time I waved my hand in the air for more tea for the *men of Ammancha.*

The three-story building in downtown Amman that housed the café was a nothing square concrete structure painted celadon, an off-color greenish blue, with large patches of flaked concrete wall. To get there, you had to walk down a small alleyway past a falafel stand, go left, and then follow the arrow upstairs. The passageway looked like every crowded corridor in every North African city in every *Jason Bourne* movie ever made. Through a second-floor doorway, a grand room opened up, revealing tables and chairs scattered across a light-blue linoleum floor that extended out to the terrace.

I'm guessing, but I believed they stopped making that color of flooring. Allah was merciful.

Everyone seated was with someone else. Men drinking tea and smoking cigarettes conversed in low tones. There were no women. The third floor was reserved for them. Ancient lands sometimes clung to old rules, which later formed inexplicable habits.

I avoided juxtaposing my own pop-cultural values against a region whose culture had an eight-thousand-year head start on mine. It bought them some leeway, to my thinking. It was impossible to overlook that the Tigris and Euphrates Rivers were within a day's ride to the northeast. Words I had never had the chance to work into a sentence before outside of history class, like *Mesopotamia*, *Assyria*, and *Phoenicia*, suddenly became part of morning small talk with Horse of God.

I had staked out a small table and seat at the edge of the balcony directly above the traffic mayhem two stories below. From where I sat, I watched as streams of cars, trucks, and mopeds rumbled down King Hussein Street headed south, where they met with traffic moving east and west across Shabaan Street and King Faisal Square. The confluence of the traffic, like too much bad cholesterol, eventually strangled the flow, until the entire mess came to a standstill as if paralyzed by a stroke.

From where I sat, if you walked about a mile up King Hussein Street, you'd find the Caravan Hotel on the corner of Abdali and al-Maamoun Streets. I lived there. It was more of a bed-and-breakfast than a hotel, but I wasn't going to quibble with Ali al-Shorman over the finer points of the hospitality industry. Mostly, my morning constitutional meant walking a mile or so for tea, a newspaper, and a cigarette. It was on one of those mornings that I met Horse of God.

Everyone has a rituals to start their day. Coffee. Tea. Shower. Shave. Toothbrush. Bagels. Croissants. TV morning news. Toast. Newspaper. Whatever. When I am away, my morning routine creates a sense of belonging and even a contrived sense of home. In the absence of truth, illusions provide comfort.

In Honolulu, my life had been on autopilot. Without a second thought, I could get to my grocery store, drugstore, bank, café, movie theater, 7-Eleven, post office, and dry cleaner, and any other of the myriad of places I had catalogued in my head that made me feel the familiarity I identified generally as *home*.

I've been away from home a lot during my life, so small rituals are important. Mostly, when I was away from home, I tried to awaken the same way, with a coffee and a newspaper. One time I was on assignment in a war zone in East Timor. I still managed to find a cup of joe and a newspaper. Even if the paper was written in four different languages—Bahasa Indonesian, Tetum, Portuguese, and English—it was still a newspaper. My sense of home in East Timor came in multiple languages.

When I was in Islamabad, my breakfast coffee was strong and dark and the newspaper mystifying. The Land of the Pure uses 622 CE as its day one, the year of the migration of Mohammed from Mecca to Medina. That placed me squarely in Pakistan's capital city in 1425 of the Hijri calendar. My Muslim home was in the fifteenth century.

As is the case for the Japanese, my morning repast in Kyoto was simultaneously simpler and more complicated. Coffee was Illy brand from Italy. But the year was 27 of the reign of Emperor Akihito of the Heisei Era, son of Hirohito, posthumously named Emperor Shōwa. There's no place like *hōmu*.

I bought my coffee and pastry in the same shop along King Hussein Street until the clerks began to recognize me. "As-salaam alaikum!" one would say to greet me. At some magical moment I became a regular customer.

The pastry choices didn't seem as bewildering as they had been at first, and I now knew the prices. The transaction was reduced to relative effortlessness. Home was life on autopilot again, except now it was in the Middle East. These were the kinds of little things that made me feel as if I was a part of the community instead of being on the outside looking in.

With familiarity came ease and the comfort to laugh at myself as I shamelessly tried to use the halting expressions taken from the "Useful Phrases" section of my *Arabic Pocket Dictionary*. More often than not, my miscues opened the door for the other person to attempt to speak English learned mostly from US TV shows and movies.

A bus driver in Palankaraya, Central Kalimantan, Borneo, once asked me whether all Americans talked to their cars. Apparently, he had learned some of his English from watching David Hasselhoff's character converse with his artificially intelligent 1982 Pontiac Trans-Am known as "Kitt" on the hit TV show *Knight Rider*.

I had a very long conversation once with a Tibetan monk in Dharamsala, India, about *Spiderman*.

At least anecdotally, I submit from personal experience that Hollywood may have a greater impact on international perceptions of the United States than it realizes. The good work of the Peace Corps and USAID programs aside, they can't begin to compete with, say, *Iron Man*.

"No. I'm sorry," I expressed, to the apparent disappointment my Dayak bus driver in Borneo, "Americans do not talk with their cars like that."

"No. I'm sorry, Tenzin Kalsang B," I disclosed, "there were a lot of special effects in that movie."

These experiences of curiosity and, at times, shared laughter were what built my sense of connection locally. Every routine, each personal exchange, each question about the United States and Americans answered, demystified caricatures and cultivated a feeling of acceptance. At some vague point in time, wherever I was became where I lived.

Horse of God's friendship dropped me into Amman's community as if I were a native son returning home. We both acted like we had always been here, instead of he being an Iraqi expatriate and I being a hapless rambler with little regard for a world with borders.

Horse of God was a youthful sixty-something. I'm not sure he even had a copy of his Iraqi birth certificate to check. Regardless, he was as restless and as dynamic as a waterfall: always opining, walking, drinking, smoking, painting, and laughing. We met regularly and often for breakfast and sometimes dinner. Invariably, his daily routine forced him back to his studio to paint in the early afternoon at his house near the ancient Roman Temple of Hercules.

One day, while sharing tea, he asked me if I wanted to see some of his paintings.

"Hell yes!" I exclaimed. "Let's go!"

"Okay! We go for-r-r taxi!" he announced, darting up from our table while still talking. On Shabaan Street, we grabbed one. Horse of God growled something in Arabic just before we sped off. We drove through a series of back streets until we pulled up in front of the Jordan National Gallery of Fine Arts.

"Salaam!" he said while waving his hand in a circle. He grumbled something in his gravelly voice as he walked toward the glass front doors. I ran in front him, grabbed one of the doors, and yanked it open.

"Really?" I blurted, as Horse of God walked past me. Translated into Arabic, it means, of course, "Really?"

He marched into the atrium, offered a blessing to a young woman at the counter where we were supposed to purchase an entrance ticket, and just kept on walking.

"As-salaam alaikum!" I uttered to the young lady. "I'm with him!" I added, pointing at his back.

I followed Horse of God down a hall. After some lefts and rights, there we stood in front of two large paintings by Mohammed Muhraddin. It was like a reenactment of a scene from *Ferris Bueller's Day Off*, the one where Ferris, Sloane, and Cameron pop into the Chicago Art Institute to pass a portion of the day as part of their truancy from school. But instead of standing in front of George Seurat's iconic pointillist painting *A Sunday Afternoon on the Island of La Grande Jatte*, we were staring at Horse of God's work.

I looked over at Horse of God as he stood there silently, like he was seeing the paintings for the first time and was trying to figure out what the artist was trying to say. They were beautiful mixed-media images with textures; vibrant colors; scribbles of letters, numbers, and words; paper with torn edges; and geometric lines confronted by wild scratches. To name-drop, his work has been exhibited in London, Paris, Cannes, Cairo, Ankara, and Washington, DC.

While standing there, Horse of God said nothing about his paintings. He would push his glasses up onto his forehead and perch them there. Then he would approach his paintings and get within inches of the surface as if he had spotted something out of place. Seconds later he would step back and pull his glasses back down onto the bridge of his nose.

"Okay?" he said once he was satisfied.

It wasn't a question, even though it sounded like one.

"We go now!" he thundered with a smile.

"You're a terrible docent, Horse of God," I said, throwing my arm over his shoulder as we turned away.

But Horse of God was a great tour guide. We walked out of the Jordan National Gallery of Fine Arts, made a right, and within a few minutes were eating sandwiches and drinking on the *terrazza* at the Canvas Café Restaurant and Art Lounge. It was a picturesque day. A robin's-egg-blue sky was overhead, there was luminous sunshine and a cool breeze, and Horse of God and I were content, feeling that life couldn't get any better.

After attending the museum and having some drinks, and perhaps while still drunk, Horse of God took me to a Jordan Telecom Group store, where I bought a Nokia mobile phone for JOD25, a SIM card for JOD15, and some minutes. It wasn't my idea. Horse of God had decided that I needed a mobile phone so he could call me to set up our meetings. Soon thereafter he would call me at random times to offer unsolicited opinions.

"R-r-rock Hudson, the best Amer-r-rican actor-r-r ever-r-r!" he bellowed.

Click.

"Do you know this movie *Amadeus*? Fantastic! Fantastic!" he would roar, without ever identifying himself.

Click.

He wasn't rude. Not in the least. He was the opposite, in fact. When he had something to say, he said it, and then it was time to go back to painting or drinking or eating or sleeping. He was always contemplating the curious thought of how he could touch other human beings with his shapes and colors and numbers and scribbles.

He lived like I strived to live: immediate, present, always full of ideas.

Horse of God thought a cell phone was important for me because there were no such things as public telephones in Jordan. That fact notwithstanding, and while in a state of mild inebriation, that was how I ended up with a registered Jordanian mobile number—thanks to Horse of God's Amman address. As I walked out of the store with my Nokia, I told Horse of God I didn't know anyone in Amman but him.

I was wrong. Horse of God wasn't the only one who would call. Without realizing it, I had acquired a diverse set of Iraqi, Jordanian, and Lebanese friends. In spite of my passport, I now lived in Amman. And further, I apparently liked to talk to people, even if I tortured their language horribly in the process.

Nadia, director of Lines Contemporary Art Gallery, called to invite both of us to an art exhibition. A few of Horse of God's pieces would be on display.

Hamden, a taxi driver, called to confirm a date and time for my trip to Wadi Rum from Aqaba.

Saed, founder of the Institute for Arabian Horsemanship, called to confirm my interview with him. *Arabian Horse Magazine* later ran a story I wrote entitled "Knights of the Wind: The Art of Arabian Horsemanship Lives Again."

Someone from Habibah & Sons Sweets called to tell me my gift of desserts for Horse of God and a few of his friends was ready for pickup.

Raed was an acquaintance I met at an Internet café above Shabaan Street who called to invite me to Jafra Café one night for music, for coffee, and to smoke nargeilah.

Tariq was Horse of God's friend who was a ceramist from Baghdad and who wanted to meet for coffee and practice his English.

Khaled was a Jordanian citizen assigned to the British Consulate in Amman who had family in Syria and called to make sure I had returned from Damascus safely.

It seemed I was constantly buying more minutes. Within a few weeks, I had already collected twelve Ma'ak cards, three Fastlink cards, and two Jordan Telecom Group cards. If this was what it cost to speak English in the Middle East, thank goodness I didn't speak Arabic.

After a few weeks in Amman, I felt the need to run away from home. I asked Ali if I could leave some belongings at the Caravan while I went south to Aqaba and then into the Red Desert.

"Yes, Mister Guy! Inshallah, we will keep your room for you!"

I promised to return within a few weeks. Inshallah.

In spite of Horse of God's objections, I left Amman to become a bedouin. He'd had enough of the desert sand while in Basra and Baghdad. Horse of God was now a city dweller and loved everything the city had to offer. He loved the art. He loved good food and strong drinks. He loved innocent flirting with pretty women. He loved to laugh loudly. He loved to sit and opine about politics. He loved to discuss history and music and philosophy. I left all of that and headed for the sand.

WADI RUM: IN THE VALLEY OF THE MOON

Of all the people I knew who should question my decision to go into the Red Desert, I thought Horse of God had the most right to so. On a superficial level, I say that because he grew up surrounded by sand in Iraq. When he went off to Poland to study art, he returned a full-fledged desert deserter. Like a reformed cigarette smoker, he was most severe with those who still wanted to smoke.

On a visceral level, it was more than just sand; it was the idea of going away to a place where nothing is what a person did there. *That* concept he apparently couldn't grasp. "Why you go ther-r-re?" he boomed. "Ther-r-re is nothing! Her-r-re is everything!" he proclaimed.

True. Wadi Rum is pretty much 278 square miles of empty space. It could fit vacantly inside of Rhode Island three times. Why then leave all of the amenities of Amman, where there were endless charming distractions?

The reply "Why not?" is little more than a dodge. At best it represented lazy thinking. The truth of it is, every so often, nothing is enough for me. Life isn't only a series of food and drink and conversation and film and artwork and music. Sometimes it's the pause, the absence, the interval between things that makes way for awareness to enter.

Routines have never made anyone's life interesting. Instead, I seek the yin and the yang, the contribution of opposites to make a complete whole. It was living in a longhouse with the headhunters of Borneo in the moist heat of the tropics one year and then living at −25°C at the foot of K2 in another. It was running from a charging bull elephant in Botswana because I was in the wrong place and then preparing a Thanksgiving feast with my Italian friends in Vicenza, Italy, because that was precisely where I wanted to be. It was eating sushi in Tsukiji, Tokyo, and pork barbeque in North Carolina. Balance.

And then I sometimes needed *nothing* to counterbalance all that something. When I took a breather, I allowed myself to consider where I was, what I was doing, and who was around me. In the quiet moments, I could focus on the present rather than always wondering, *What's next?* Simply put, *doing nothing is doing something.*

With that in mind, I said to Horse of God, "To do absolutely nothing for a while." And that, surprisingly, seemed to please him.

I didn't know what to expect when I arrived in Wadi Rum. What I did know made me sound like a hack film critic. I knew that the Oscar-winning film *Lawrence of Arabia* (1963) starring Peter O'Toole was filmed there.

I also knew it carried the moniker "the Red Desert." But how expansive and red can sand be? Red. And expansive. When I got to our campsite, the vision of red sand extending into the horizon explained why Hollywood sought Wadi Rum for science fiction films such as *The Red Planet, Prometheus, The Last Days of Mars,* and most recently, *The Martian.*

My journey to Mars began humbly with me grabbing a taxi to Wahadat Station in southern Amman to board a bus to Aqaba. The system for transport in Jordan is fairly self-evident. If you want to go north, you go to the bus station in the northern part of the city. For the south, you go to the southern station.

When I arrived at Wahadat Station, I discovered that getting a ticket was going to be another adventure altogether. There were plenty of buses, but no signs indicating which buses went where. Let me re-phrase that. There were plenty of signs if you could read Arabic.

There wasn't a central ticket office, which meant there also wasn't a place to find a full schedule of departures. I did surmise through trial and error that each bus was operated privately and so each coach had its own ticket office and departure timetable. Some days, life presented greater adventures than on other days.

"As-salaam alaikum!" I began. This was followed quickly by, "*Ana asif!*" (I'm sorry!) "*Aqaba min fadlak?*" (Aqaba, please?)

Fingers pointed.

Then other fingers pointed.

And more pointed.

Finally, I exchanged some Jordanian dollars for a small piece of paper that represented my passage south.

Several air-condition-less hours later, I arrived in Aqaba, Jordan's resort on the Red Sea. I grabbed my shoulder bag from the luggage compartment below and went in search of a roof and a bed. In the unpredictability that insinuates itself most days into my unplanned travel, I chanced upon al-Kholi Hotel near one of the souks. I en-tered, walking across the lobby to the front desk. Here's my actual exchange with the clerk:

> Desk clerk: As-salaam alaikum!
> Me: Wa alaikum salaam!
> Desk clerk: You want room?

Me: Na'am, min fadlak.

Desk clerk: Okay. I have room.

Me: Shukran!

Desk clerk: You want pay now?

Me: Uh, I think I need to change money first.

Desk clerk: Okay. You pay now.

Me: Okay. I'll pay now.

Desk clerk: Okay. You pay later.

Me: Shukran!

At this point it, was obvious that one or perhaps both of us were engaged in a nearly futile act of communication. Usually my fallback position was to smile and wait. When he turned to give me my room key, the conversation crystalized: I would pay later.

After dropping my bag off in my room, I walked out of the hotel and down to the beach, still perplexed but happy I had a home. From this one beautiful spot on the Jordanian Red Sea coastline, I heard the waves rushing slowly to shore while gazing at Israel and Egypt. Even though Saudi Arabia was less than a day's camel ride away to the south, a beach is a beach. Suddenly I felt at home.

Living in Honolulu meant I was always close to the water. If I wasn't physically in the ocean, I could still see it. It was everywhere, so ubiquitous that at times I overlooked the fact that over one-third of the planet's surface was right there all around me. Some things are so large you can't see them.

I awoke early the following day. Hamden N'imat arrived to take me due east. After about an hour's drive, I paid JOD2 for a pass to enter the Wadi Rum Protected Area. In the village within, I met Madallah Atiq, who had been referred to me by Hamden. I suspected from their greeting that either Hamden and Madallah were related or some baksheesh was about to exchange hands.

Madallah handed me his card, which read," Bedween [sic] guide." Being not so great a speller myself, I didn't read too much into that. But in case all else failed, I had brought my Boy Scout compass.

We waited a while until his nephew Mohammed Zarabia drove up in a banged-up jeep. Shortly thereafter, Mohammed and I sped off into the desert in a cloud of dust. Mohammed was a bedouin even though he wore camouflage pants and sported a Yankees baseball cap. We drove for about an hour or so before pulling up behind a sandstone outcropping with several tents perched at its foot. I helped Mohammed unload our water, food, and gear.

"People who come now don't respect desert," Mohammed expressed with a hint of melancholy. "It is my home, but they are not quiet," he observed. Mohammed had served in the Jordanian army for two years but could not wait to return to this vast expanse of dryness.

Once things at camp appeared to be sorted out, he grabbed a shovel from one of the tents and began digging a pit about a meter deep and half a meter across. Then he stuffed kindling under some sunbaked wood and struck a match. In seconds, a fire began to rage in the hole.

After the flames reduced to embers, Mohammed arranged the embers to his liking. On top of a grill lowered into the hole about a foot above the coals, Mohammed placed chicken seasoned with olive oil, paprika, salt, pepper, and curry spices, along with onions and potatoes. He covered the food with a metal lid and buried everything in the sand. This was a *zarb*.

After dinner was buried, Mohammed built another fire in a shallow pit in front of the main tent and began preparing tea with cardamom pods and sugar. He disappeared momentarily inside his tent and then returned with a lute. He tuned it by ear and, when satisfied, began strumming.

"Life without love is like a river without water," he sang. I was once told while traveling in sub-Saharan Africa that it is better to see with your head and to hear with your heart. This seemed to apply here.

The verses sung by Mohammed were particularly apropos considering we were encamped in Wadi Rum, which means "River of

Sand." While Mohammed sang of lost love, I sat on the shoreline of sand and imagined a river flowing by.

Mohammed's lute was as Arabian as he was. Along with the Quran, the North African Moors had brought a fretless instrument called an oud and their keen sense of harmony to the Iberian Peninsula in the early eighth century. When the Christians wrested Spain from the Moors seven hundred years later, the Spaniards exported what became a five-stringed instrument with frets known for all the European rage as a lute. Sometime in the seventeenth century, the Italians added a sixth string.

Thus, the world was at least partially indebted to our Islamic friends for contributing to the development of what we now know as the guitar. Americans, however, never ones to leave a good thing alone, added electricity. As a consequence, and as much as part of the Arab world would like to distance itself from anything remotely identified with the West, were it not for the reach of the Arab civilization into the Iberian Peninsula, bands like the Beatles, the Rolling Stones, and the Who might not have been possible nearly twelve hundred years later.

Mohammed paused. In the silence we heard the clamber of an ailing truck pull up to our camp, which was now engulfed in darkness. Tashmir, Mohammed's bedouin cousin, emerged and entered camp, shouting as if he were a night marauder. He feigned an attack and then gently approached Mohammed. Tashmir greeted his relative warmly by kissing him first on his left cheek once and then three times on his right shoulder.

To put the ancestors of Mohammed and Tashmir into historical perspective, I went rifling through some old maps of the world in my head and some text I had read years ago in one of my favorite books of all time, *The Columbia History of the World*, edited by John A. Garraty and Peter Gay. History had recorded the rise and fall of a myriad of empires whose armies traipsed around here, near here, and through here. The Red Desert only appeared empty because the expanse of sand seemed vacant to the eye. But the entire chronicle of the Middle East can be told by the ghosts of the armies that marched in every direction of the compass with Jordan at its center. Their footprints were once tracks in this sand.

Mohammed pulled some pillows from the tent and spread them out around the campfire so his cousin could relax comfortably. Tashmir sat with us, ate dinner, and enjoyed a pot of sweet tea. Mohammed and Tashmir talked in Arabic for a while. I let my eyes dance with the flames. Occasionally, I rose and offered everyone more tea.

After some time passed, Tashmir grabbed the lute and began singing in the poetic words of the Arabic language.

"My *habibi*, my love, you have been away so long. Now that you have returned, it is like the sun rising in the morning sky." When Tashmir finished, Mohammed and I clapped enthusiastically.

Mohammed then took up the lute and sang a song of unrequited love. I sat in silence and stared at the dancing colors of red, orange, yellow, and white from our fire. I was dozing off when I heard him strum a final chord.

While the strings were still vibrating from Mohammed's fingers, Tashmir rose, strode across the sand to his cousin, lifted the lute from him, and came over to present it to me. Not a word was spoken.

"Ana asif!" I pleaded, telling him that I was sorry. Apparently and without warning, it was my turn to play. I tried desperately to beg off. Wordlessly I expressed, "I don't know how to play this."

Tashmir would have none of it. He resolutely held the lute by its neck, suspending it out in front of me as if it were a gift I couldn't refuse.

"And I really can't sing," I continued futilely.

There was a long pause as he stood. I looked at Mohammed, who was looking back at me.

"Okay!" I said, not wishing to cause an international incident by appearing rude. I acquiesced in spite of all my nonartistic instincts otherwise.

"You have been warned!" I declared, now embarrassed by my earlier refusal and in anticipation of my performance to come.

Then with a soft yellow moonglow reflecting off of distant Al Qattara mountain in the great emptiness of the Jordanian Sahara, and with the eyes of the only two people I knew for hundreds of miles focused on me, I engaged in what could only be described as bedouin karaoke. I took a halting breath in reluctant preparation. Then I began to sing the words and melody of the only song I could remember under such pressure, "Waikīkī."

"There's a feeling deep in my heart," I began tentatively, "stabbing at me just like a dart ..."

And drowning in the pure anxiety of the moment, I couldn't for the life of me remember the rest of the introduction. Nothing. Zip. So I did what Justin Timberlake suggested to do in *Sexyback*: I took 'em to the bridge.

"Ohhhhhhhhhhhhhh Waikīkī," I wailed, "at night when the shadows are falling, I hear your rolling surf calling, calling, and calling to me!"

And so it went.

As out of place as it may have been to sing of my home by the sea, my rendition proved to be even more appalling than I can fully express. Comforted only in the thought that Mohammed and Tashmir didn't know the actual lyrics or melody, I steeled myself as best I could and had at it full-throttle, full-throated, all-in. Audaciously, I served up every off-key note, every missed verse, every jumbled phrase. My sincere apologies to Andy Cummings.

Somehow, mercifully, I got to the end and let the last resonant tones of the strings expire into the Orion constellation above us. In the silence that filled the Valley of the Moon, Mohammed and Tashmir clapped joyously and hooted with glee. Each sharp whack of their hands echoed off the monstrous stone monolith standing before us in the distance. Bedouin hospitality, apparently, included uncommon kindness.

Soon after, I felt the coolness of a barren land that permitted all of the heat of the day to radiate out into the heavens. With the fire diminishing, I rose slowly, and made the universal sign for sleep. I turned and entered the tent, emerging a second later with some blankets under my arm. Earlier, I had spotted a small sand dune nearby rising to a plateau. I chose that as my bedroom for the night.

Mohammed talked for a while with Tashmir. As I settled in, I could feel the chill of the desert night on my cheeks. Never underestimate the temperature of the desert at night by considering the heat you feel during the day. The solar warmth contained in the sand radiated swiftly away. With the autumn's cool winds marauding down from the hills of Turkey, I pulled the hood of my North Face windbreaker over my head and tucked my legs and chest under two blankets.

My eyes scanned the blackness of the bedouin sky above. Astrophysicists have suggested that the needlepoints of light from the nearest stars are already four years old. But light from stars emanating from across our galaxy is over one hundred thousand years old. The thought of all of that ancient radiance made me feel both old and young at the same time. For Einstein, I'm sure he'd say simply: "It's all relative."

I watched shooting stars fall into my hair. There were streaks to the east. Others flashed brilliantly as they faded to the west. A white stripe plunged into my boots. And sometime in the course of the night, safe and warm, I fell asleep in the River of Sand.

"Marhaba! Marhaba!" woke everyone the following morning at camp. The shouts came from Haled, who had just arrived on camelback with one in tow. Colloquially, the word was used as hello. Some linguists claim that the word derives from a Persian word conveying the message "No harm can come from me to you!" New Age dictionaries tout *Marhaba!* as "God is love!"

To me, it meant breakfast.

"Marhaba!" I rasped in my morning voice as I rolled over. Mohammed had risen before dawn and had already stoked the fire from the coals the night before. Soon thereafter we were all sitting around the fire drinking sweet tea and eating hard-boiled eggs with flatbread.

"I am all broken," Haled complained, wincing and smiling at the same time. He shifted from side to side as if to make a point. "My bottom broken, my stomach broken. Bedouin life hard!"

I hold no opinions on Haled's last two claims, but I did have a fairly solid scientific explanation for why his backside hurt.

In appearance alone, pretty much everyone agrees that camels are physiological oddities of nature. Evolution resulted in an adaptation to desert terrain, where camel feet flattened out nearly to the size of an elephant's foot to act like snowshoes on sand. Rather than plunging deep into the dunes with every step, they could now move easily across the shifting surface.

The camel also modified how it walked. Only the equally odd-looking llama joined with the camel to traverse across the earth ipsilaterally, that is, by moving both of the right appendages forward first and then both of the left ones. Hence, the rocking motion.

This made sense, even if it did so at the expense of the rider's comfort. Unlike horses or dogs, which use a diagonal cross-motion between the front and opposing rear appendages, camels apparently have figured out that they can extend their front and rear legs further in one motion by throwing both out at the same time. Scientists have confirmed that by moving in this way, ipsilateral creatures can cover more ground using less energy than their other four-legged cousins. This is a practical adaptation when you consider the lack of food and water available in Wadi Rum and other places like it.

Camels are good for other things too, like milk. Camel's milk to be exact.

"You drink milk of camel?" Haled asked me, as if such was what normal morning conversation entailed.

"Camel milk!" he repeated. "You drink?"

"I don't think so," I said sheepishly. "Is it good for you?"

"Bedouin drink camel's milk with honey in morning," he disclosed.

Haled, Tashmir, and Mohammed smiled at one another. Everyone knows that any group of guys smiling at one another, regardless of culture, means that something is going down.

"It natural Viagra!" Haled shouted as he made a fist and pointed his forearm toward the sky. With that, they all burst out laughing. Whether it is little blue pills or camel's milk, the more you travel, the more familiar everything becomes.

DAMASCUS: THE ANVIL OF BELIEFS

A week later, I returned to Amman. I called Horse of God and asked if we could meet for breakfast the next day. He was glad I had returned safely.

"You ar-r-re back fr-r-rom deser-r-rt! Good! Tomor-r-row night we go Chr-r-ristian town. Alfor-r-rhess. I call my fr-r-riend Omar-r-r Shahuan. He is painter-r-r also! We eat. Dr-r-rink beer-r-r and whis-key. We talk." *Click.*

The next evening, we did just that. We ate kabobs and vegetables and flatbread. We drank beer with whiskey. We smoked cigarettes. Later Horse of God ordered nargeilah, a water pipe about a meter tall with tobacco stuffed into a bowl carved from a fresh apple, forc-ing each puff to become infused with its natural sweetness.

We talked about art and art history; literature and life; politics and painting. When we got really drunk, we sang songs in Arabic.

"Your Ar-r-rabic is better-r-r when you ar-r-re drunk!" Horse of God decreed.

"That's because your hearing gets worse when you are drunk!" I replied.

We laughed.

We smoked.

We drank some more.

Then Horse of God and Omar began to discuss their philosophy of painting.

"When you star-r-t," Horse of God explained, "a painting is like child. It say nothing to you. But then as it gr-r-row, it make own decision.

"I star-r-rt painting," Horse of God slurred, "and make it gr-r-reen. Later-r-r it tell me it want be or-r-range! So I must make or-r-range! I cannot help it. Believe me!"

Omar and I believed him. I waved my hand in the air for three more whiskeys. "Shukran!"

"So, Horse of God," I interjected, "how do I get to Damascus?"

"What you mean?" he roared. "You ar-r-rive just now her-r-re!" He lit another cigarette.

"I know," I said, "but with all of your talk with Omar of Iraq and Syria, I want to go to see Damascus for myself."

I couldn't help my thoughts from wandering. While they were speaking, every time I heard the word *Damascus*, every imagining I had ever had of every memory of medieval tales, every history book I had ever read that spoke of the Crusades, every picture I had ever seen of knights bearing broadswords fighting men with scimitars, foot soldiers with bows and arrows, and men draped in mail engaged in desert combat, every sketch I had ever studied of the mysterious women in burqas hidden entirely from view save their penetrating eyes, every travelogue like famed adventurer Wilfred Thesiger's *Arabian Sands* or Freya Stark's revealing *Baghdad Sketches*, and every painting I had ever seen in every museum I had ever wandered through that had a Eugène Delacroix masterpiece like the *Combat of the Giour and the Pasha* came to life. None of this can begin to capture the exuberance that welled up inside of me at the thought of plunging deep into al-Hamidiyah Souk and into the heart of the old city of Damascus sheltered farther within.

Since the time I was a young boy, I had accepted movement as a basic, elemental part of what my life consisted of. So maybe, by the time I was in my forties, I was already (and permanently) hard-wired to keep pushing outward. Just the mere suggestion of a place I had not seen with my own two eyes was reason enough to begin the process of determining how to get there. *Damascus* triggered all of that and lit up my brain in the anticipation of yet another one-way ride.

"You mean al-Sham?" Horse of God said, breaking my meditation.

"Okay," I muttered in between drinks and puffs of smoke. "If that's what you call Damascus, then yes, al-Sham." For everything I thought I knew, my ignorance never ceased to surprise me.

I pulled out my map and saw that it had Damascus as *Damas* (French) and as *Dimashq* (Arabic). This was emblematic of how enchanting and intriguing, and yet bewildering, even the most banal of our conversations could become. In the span of two minutes, one ancient city was identified by words in four languages.

"When you walk down King Hussein Str-r-reet, ar-r-round the corner-r-r from wher-r-re you live, ther-r-re is taxi ser-r-rveese. Go to one Amman al-Sham, painted on door-r-r. That one to Damascus." Horse of God had already thought it through for me.

Done.

Two days later I was sitting at the taxi stand, having paid JOD9 for the front passenger seat. Then I waited. Horse of God neglected to tell me that when you travel by taxi service, the Peugeot 505 has four seats to sell. The passengers in the back sit three across, so before I could depart, I needed to wait for three more people to buy the seats going my way. Unlike what I had paid, the back seats were cheaper at JOD8 each. And it was anyone's guess if and when we would depart that day.

Thankfully, Abu Omar of Mohammed and Hamdi al-Salhi Trading Co. was headed to al-Sham on business. Then Khaled arrived at the stand and paid. The three of us waited as the midday sun rose. Finally, once our last seat was sold to a university student, we loaded our bags and sped north toward the border of the Syrian Arab Republic.

Khaled worked for the British Consulate and his English was better than mine. He was upbeat and outgoing, and although he was from Jordan, his wife's family lived in Syria. He thought it was wonderful that I was traveling to Damascus but warned me to beware once we crossed the border.

"Mister Guy," Khaled cautioned, "there are many secret police in Syria."

"Shukran!" I said a little nervously. I changed the subject to Khaled and his family.

"This is Amal," he said, joyously sharing a picture of his young daughter from his wallet. He said with obvious pride, "It means 'hope.' I think we need this now in the world."

Damascus was a little more than 100 kilometers from the Jordanian border crossing at ar-Ramtha. On this side of the border, we entered Jordanian Immigration to pay a JOD5 departure tax. Then we got back into the car and drove a few more minutes before we entered the Syrian Arab Republic Immigration Office in Daraa. There, I presented my passport and visa at the foreigners' window. When all was approved, we met back at the car and proceeded to Damascus.

Beforehand, Khaled had explained it would be simple. But when we separated at Daraa Immigration, he looked back at me as if that was the last time we would ever see each other. Syria suddenly stood poised as slightly more treacherous than I had anticipated. To be forewarned is to be forearmed.

Everyone waited for me back at the taxi, as I was the last one to be processed. Maybe someone at SAR Immigration was secretly calling the SAR secret police. As I approached them smiling, I flashed my Syrian Arab Republic visa stamp. Our driver was annoyed by the delay.

Less than two hours later, we arrived in Damascus, disembarking at a seemingly random spot along a traffic circle near the center of a sprawling metropolis. As I exited the car, I was confronted with a crush of traffic noise, cool October breezes, and a dizzying array of street vendors cooking chicken, lamb, and vegetables over glowing embers of charcoal.

Living in Amman had taught me that Arabian culture placed a significant amount of emphasis on social grace.

"Alhamdulillah!" we each declared to one another in recognition of the higher power that had allowed us to arrive safely. (Praise to Allah!) Even though we were acquainted for less than a day, as we parted, we waved goodbye as if we were good friends.

While unloading our bags, I asked Khaled if he had any suggestions for a roof over my head. He rattled off a few names. After some internal dialogue, I decided to make my home at al-Hamra Hotel. It means "the Red One" in Arabic, with *Hamra* being the root word of the Spanish translation for the spectacular citadel known as the Alhambra in Granada, Spain.

Upon arriving on the Iberian Peninsula, the Moorish emir Mohammed ben al-Ahmar rebuilt the remains of the Roman stronghold that had been abandoned there in the ninth century. After its magnificent restoration, for over four hundred years it was splendorous home sweet bayt for the ruling North African sovereignty. When the Christians wrested Spain from the Moors in the fifteenth century, King Ferdinand and Queen Isabella used the Alhambra as their royal court.

It was there that the implorations of an ambitious Italian from Genoa named Cristoforo Colombo convinced the Spanish rulers to send him off to find a shorter trade route to the islands of Japan. Cristoforo's plan was simple. He would sail due west until he ran into Japan.

In spite of what your mother told you, simpler is not always better. After sailing due west for a while, Cristoforo stumbled onto an unintended destination he modestly dubbed the New World, where they did not, by the way, speak Japanese.

Thus, in an odd twist of fate, if it weren't for the combined efforts of Roman architects, a North African Arab emir, and Spanish royalty, who knows if Amerigo Vespucci would have ever had the chance to draw an inaccurate map and credit Cristoforo Colombo with discovering America. By removing the pagan Romans, the

Muslim Moors, and the Christian Spaniards from the equation, history could have easily gone differently.

Maybe life happened a certain way because a butterfly somewhere flapped its wings and something else somewhere else happened as a result. The mere fact that I knew some purely random facts from the history of the Iberian Peninsula was enough for me to choose al-Hamra Hotel. And like Cristoforo, I did not land in Japan.

My humble al-Hamra Hotel had a fabulous pedigree in its name, but my room was no room in the Alhambra. Remember when Juliet Capulet asked in her soliloquy of her lover Romeo Montague, "What's in a name?" Well, everything sometimes. For al-Hamra Hotel, my highest expectations were met with the modest and wholly unpretentious qualities of being clean, cheap, and central. Like Cristoforo's ship, the *Santa Maria*, my Alhambra expectations ended up on the rocks.

One name did not, though, in any way, disappoint: *Damascus*.

"I'm in Damascus!" I said to myself out loud. It wasn't the factual existence of Dimashq that made it so brilliant. Rather, it was the exotic expanse of history that one simple three-syllable word triggered.

The idea that maps still designate areas in Damascus as the Jewish Quarter, the Christian Quarter, and the Muslim Quarter serves to perpetuate the marketplace of two-thousand-year-old religious ideas. Damascus endures as the anvil upon which politics and religion pound upon one another.

At the same time, Damascus had been and currently remains home to some of the loftiest aspirations of humankind. One gate in the northern portion of the old city is named Bab al-Salaam, the Gate of Peace. Like Khaled's daughter Amal, Bab al-Salaam represents hope.

For all that it symbolizes, Damascus is also much less. It is commonplace to the point of being wonderfully, unexceptionally ordinary. Stone gates that had long ago lost their purpose of protecting innocents from marauders now served to contain the clamor of shopkeepers, jewelers, clothiers, shoemakers, spice sellers, flatbread bakers, kabob grillers, pâtissiers with desserts, tea shops, coffee-houses, and every manner of daily commerce along the streets and souks, as I imagined it must have always been. In one of the oldest continuously inhabited cities in the world, today was just another day.

One afternoon well after Zuhr, the muezzin's noon call to prayer, I left my al-Hamra Hotel and cruised through Bab al-Sharqi to wander down the street called Straight. No plan. No map. No destination. I just wanted to be able to say to someone someday in the old folks' home, "I remember the day I strolled down the street called Straight in Damascus."

On the surface it seemed like not much to boast about. But it was kind of a big deal. The street called Straight was built by the Romans and is referred to in the Bible. Although the reference is biblical, the name, at best, is a misnomer.

"The street called Straight was straighter than a corkscrew but not as straight as a rainbow!" Mark Twain memorably and more accurately observed.

As I am prone to do a couple of times a day, I stumbled into a small shop with an "As-salaam alaikum!" and ordered a Turkish coffee. While sipping a strong brew of *Coffea arabica* on a mild autumn day and people-watching, I flipped my journal open and wrote, "October 21 – Damascus." *Carpe diem.*

I spent the remainder of the afternoon walking aimlessly and doing little else but observing street life. At some point, I got hungry and ambled over to a small stand preparing *schawarma*. I took my place in line. Soon it was my turn.

"As-salaam alaikum! Wahid min fadlak! Shukran!" I said, and I wasn't even drunk. (The blessings of God be upon you! One, please! Thank you!)

"Na'am!" the cook replied, smiling broadly, so I knew he knew what I had just said: "Yes!" A minute later, I was sitting at a plastic table on a rickety plastic stool scarfing down the best lamb schawarma I had had since the Restaurant Fayrouz in Cotonou.

Content, I strolled through Souk al-Hamidiyah and in less than fifteen minutes, stepped into a public square fronting the Umayyad Mosque. It was a night carnival of activity. There was loud music, string lights, food stalls, children at play, moms and dads pushing infants in strollers, old men walking arm in arm talking with their hands and shuffling their feet, boys flirting with girls, girls acting like they didn't see the boys, shoppers carrying all kinds of household goods, and of course, the scent of strong coffee.

In Damascus, icons of Islamic, Christian, Jewish, and pagan creeds all coexist shoulder-to-shoulder. For me, the mosque framed the perplexing historical context of conquest, reconquest, and the influence of religion in the Middle East. Damascus confirmed that history couldn't be measured simply by counting planetary revolutions around the sun.

Once you discard time as a linear concept, you can also abandon the assumption that events that occurred thousands of years ago were rendered irrelevant by the mounting collection of ticks of a clock. Instead, by eliminating the idea of time as a limiting factor, the power of belief unleashes the believer from any separation between the then and the now.

I walked toward the main entrance of the mosque unaware of the depth of the beauty shielded within. The huge wooden medieval entranceway doors were an iconic reminder that this house of worship had been here since the early seventh century.

Once inside, I was directed politely to a ticket counter. I paid fifty Syrian pounds to a young man, was handed ticket, and strolled over to an area to remove and store my shoes. There were hundreds of pairs of shoes, mostly sandals, all clean and neatly placed along rows and rows of wooden shoe racks. I slid my Vasques onto one shelf thinking that if this wasn't a sign that a foreigner, an 'ajanbi, was in the house, then nothing was. In my bare feet, I entered the main square tiled in marble so stunningly clean and shiny that it looked wet.

Built by Caliph al-Walid ben Abdul Malek, the Ummayad Mosque is considered to be one of the most beautiful and perfect houses of prayer in the entire Islamic world. Four symmetrical walls bind the interior courtyard. The horseshoe archways that stretch along all four lengths of the interior walls left me with the impression of the Piazza San Marco in Venice.

It is common knowledge that Muslim architects applied mathematical symmetry and repetitive patterns as part of their aesthetic. Overlooking the main courtyard was a mosaic made of gold. This mosque was once home to the largest gold mosaic in the world, measuring over forty thousand square feet. The huge open courtyard over which it towers leads to long porticos, which front the main prayer hall. Here, open to the air and cool to the touch, I walked along in my bare feet proud that we, as humans, are capable of such magnificence.

In the shadows of minarets and archways, families sat together quietly, children played tag, men conversed in low tones, others read, and some milled around alone in their thoughts. The near silence was in stark, wondrous contrast to the commotion of commerce just on the other side of the walls.

After I wandered and sat and scribbled notes into my book, I exited as I had entered. When I did, I watched as an unending stream of Muslim faithful came to view the sepulcher of their great general Sahaladin and his wife, Ismat ad-Din, "Purity of the Faith."

The death of Sahaladin, or as he is known in the Islamic world, Salah al-Din Yusuf ibn Ayyub, "Righteousness of the Faith, Joseph, son of Job," at the end of the twelfth century is as a current an event today in Damascus as if it had happened yesterday. The Sahaladin mausoleum is adjacent to the mosque, and the throng of visitors paying homage did so as if Sahaladin were lying in state. A true believer's belief is not linear.

In this way, Damascus lived unenviably and simultaneously

in the present and in the ancient, as the two are inseparable here. You may hold an iPhone in your hand, but your feet fall upon stones set by Roman hands twenty-five hundred years ago. The newspapers report that today was both 2007 and 1428. Such is Damascus's plague.

It was not just the old and new that generated bewilderment. Damascus was where, *is* where, the Quran, the Bible, and the Torah all occupy space, sometimes adjacent to one another. This juggling of beliefs is not contemporary news. On Friday, certain businesses run with half their staff because their Muslim workers are at the mosque on their holy day. On Sunday, other places are run with half their staff because the Christians are in church. While most, if not all, of the Jewish community long ago fled to nearby Israel, one particular Jewish patron remains sacredly memorialized.

Consider that the glorious Umayyad Mosque is not only one of the oldest mosques in the world but also stands rather curiously as the guardian of the shrine to a Jew named John the Baptist, who later was revered as a Christian martyr and a celebrated saint. There's a lot ground to be plowed there.

Here's the *Abbreviated Religious History of Damascus for Dummies* as it relates to this period of antiquity. Our story begins as the legions of Rome fought the Persians to a draw about two thousand years ago. When the Romans took control, they imported their polytheistic beliefs and built a temple in honor of Jupiter, the king of all the gods.

Meanwhile, a Jew named John the Baptist lived part time on the street called Straight and baptized someone named Jesus. Later, John talked some trash about the pagan Roman ruler King Herod because King Herod had committed adultery with his brother's wife, Herodias.

King Herod made a bad situation worse by marrying her. John voiced his unkind moral disapproval to King Herod, who, pissed off by it all, commanded that John be separated from his head. Given John's on-and-off residence in Damascus, the Muslims felt obligated to maintain a shrine to John the Baptist within the main prayer hall of the mosque.

We can all agree that the Herod–John the Baptist story is not *Star Trek*. But still it's quite an amazing narrative: John was a Jew who became a Christian and then became dead by the pagan King Herod in a city full of Muslims who maintain a shrine to his Christian memory.

Damascus does enjoy the kind of context you can't make up. Amman notwithstanding, how many times have you ever prefaced a night out with, "Excuse me, I'm looking for some alcohol. Can you point me in the direction of the Christian Quarter?" While never appropriate, let alone necessary, under any conceivable circumstances at home, that is an entirely acceptable prelude to an evening out in Damascus if you're a tourist.

Aside from the marvel of nearly constant discovery, one of the other great pleasures of travel was meeting local residents. I encountered people all the time. I met folks while walking, or sharing a table with a stranger over Turkish coffee. The delightful result was that oftentimes I was pushed in a direction that was not initially a bearing on my compass. That was how I ended up at Beit al-Mamlouka, a boutique hotel in the Christian Quarter. Sometimes the path chooses you.

Beit al-Mamlouka is a resplendent oasis of sublime Middle Eastern art and textiles. It is also a hidden treasure. I do not mean that in the romantic sense of the expression. I mean exactly that: it is buried amid five thousand years of streets with no names. You'd think after all that time that something called a street sign would have found its place in any one of the ancient empires that ruled Damascus. It hasn't.

To give you an idea of how fun it was to find Beit al-Mamlouka, these are the actual directions I was given from the clerk at al-Hamra Hotel:

> You know Umayyad Mosque? Go to mosque. Don't go in mosque. Walk to back of mosque, where is

Roman arch. Look up to see minaret away from mosque. Walk to minaret. Then go straight. Road will split. Go left. Then road go straight. Go next left. Go until Hammam Bakri. You are there. If you see Elyssar Restaurant, you are lost.

I was lost before I even began. But no new worlds were ever discovered with one foot on the dock and one foot on the boat, so out the door I went.

I decided also that I needed some high-tech help in this very ancient place. I headed directly over to an MTN Mobile Phone Center, opened up an Areeba account, got a SIM card for my Nokia, and bought some minutes. If I was going to get lost, I wanted to be able to call someone to get me unlost. In less than an hour I had a registered Syrian mobile number.

As you might imagine, at every intersection I did what I did best: I asked for directions. Eventually a small miracle resulted. I was looking at a little brass sign that read, Beit al-Mamlouka. I banged on a huge old wooden door held together with what looked like iron railroad spikes.

"*Beit al-Mamlouka* means 'House of the Slaves,'" explained May Mamarbachi, owner and visionary of the first boutique hotel in Damascus. "I named it after the Mamluks," she said, "who were the slave class of Egypt in the thirteenth century but [who] then rose to rule as kings over much of the region that is now known as Jordan, Syria, Palestine, and Israel."

We talked in the central courtyard of what was once a private Damascene home built in the mid-1700s. May's family was from Aleppo in the north, but she wanted to do something special in Damascus. The word *special* does not do justice to what she had accomplished.

"Perfection," May declared, "is in the details." Thus, it came as no surprise when I found exquisite sweets from Ghraoui, master Arab chocolatier, on the bedside table. There were sumptuously rich sheets made of Arabian cotton tucked across a king-size bed. I slid under lavishly woven silk brocade manufactured in Damascus by the world-renowned Manzanar family. Farewell al-Hamra.

The Syrian Desert has besieged Damascus since the days of its first inhabitants. On a windy day, fine granules of sand hang suspended in midair, giving the city a pale cast of brownish gray. Within the walls of the air-conditioned Suleiman Suite, I found it easy to grasp the idea that there was nothing more luxurious than water; it came with its own fountain and rose petals floating across its surface. I felt like an oil sheik on holiday.

Holidays, though, come to an end. And with the end of my holiday came an end to my time in Damascus.

Stirred by little more than caprice, I departed Damascus for Aleppo early one Tuesday morning around 7:30. Following the same system I had used in Amman, I grabbed a taxi to Harasta Karaj, the bus station in the northern part of the city, and bought passage north. Al-Sham to Aleppo was about 350 kilometers, and ultimately the ride by Pullman bus was pretty comfortable. Think Greyhound.

While waiting to depart, I considered that I had no real reason to go to Aleppo aside from a desire to continue moving forward. May's family was from Aleppo, and she spoke of the city's history and beauty with affection. I didn't know anyone there. I didn't have a good handle on Aleppo's history except some vague notion that at one time the ancient city-states of Aleppo and Damascus competed for control of this region along the Mediterranean. Then again, this type of unpredictable behavior on my part was typical. Ask my mother.

All of my one-way train tickets, bus receipts, ferryboat vouchers, and airplane boarding passes were emblems of what my freedom looked like. I rarely knew where I was going next, when I would return, or by what means. My one-ways dared fate. I would return if and when the next one-way was the one way back. Until then, it was ever one way forward.

TO ALEPPO AND PALMYRA

[Author's Note: I could not have imagined back in the fall of 2007 that the northern and eastern regions of the Syrian Arab Republic through which I traversed would soon devolve into an all-out civil war. Neither the wonderful inhabitants of bustling Aleppo nor the quiet bedouin in the village surrounding the majestic architectural remnants of the Palmyrene Empire could have predicted the vast and nearly complete destruction of their homeland. The loss of irreplaceable structures and invaluable ancient artwork aside, it is gut-wrenching to witness a peaceful civilian population being subjected to the kinds of war crimes and indiscriminate violence that has befallen the Syrians.

This tragedy seems particularly ironic given that such uncivilized conduct has erupted within portions of Syria, Iraq, and Iran once denoted in history books as the "cradle of civilization." This is not to ignore that ancient history is replete with invading armies from the likes of the Babylonians, the Hittites, the Greeks under Alexander the Great, the Persians under Darius I, and many others. But the level of destruction we are witnessing today, given the explosive power of the ordinance being deployed, overwhelms any comparable destructive force used by the armies of Babylon or Greece or Persia.

Given what has transpired over the last five years, I feel fortunate to have wandered the glorious passageways of Aleppo and the resplendent Syrian Desert. I suspect it may be a generation before that territory is once again the treasure it used to be.]

I plopped down into a bus seat. Next to me was Mohammed Motaz al-Maradin.

"As-salaam alaikum!" I began. "My name is Guy."

"Wa alaikum salaam!" Motaz replied. And then he asked, "You are American?" in English as clear as mine.

"Yes, I am from America," I continued while extending my hand. "Actually I am from Honolulu. Do you know this place?"

Pause. "I have seen this place on TV and in movies. It is beautiful. Inshallah, God willing, I will visit one day!" he said with a broad smile.

"Hope so, Motaz. I think you would like it." And then my curiosity overwhelmed my manners. "Motaz," I said sheepishly, "may I know why your English is so good?"

"Thank you, Mr. Guy! Yes." Politely he said, "I went to school in Virginia for two years to train as an aircraft mechanic. I think now, I have forgotten too much English."

"Not at all," I reassured him.

"And you are welcome to Syria, Mr. Guy! The people, they are very nice in my country." Motaz eliminated my initial concern about secret police. Then again, maybe he was the secret police.

We spoke of family and travel and his return home to help his parents, get married, and raise a family. Simple dreams, like those of everyone everywhere I have ever met. We are all the same simple people who happen to live in different places, speak different languages, and worship differently.

Soon enough, the bus pulled into Aleppo. Motaz and I exchanged cell numbers and bid each other farewell. "Inshallah!" God willing, we would meet again. After a brief walk from the station, I found myself standing on a curb near the old walled city with my map turned upside down. It was clear to a blind man that I was lost.

Like the tourists I often saw wandering around downtown Honolulu searching for ʻIolani Palace or the King Kamehameha statue, today I was that lost tourist. Knowing that feeling of total confusion, I never hesitated to walk over to someone, introduce myself, and ask if I could help them in their search for whatever they were searching for.

Like all travelers, my experience has shown me that karma does loop back at some time. In Aleppo, that providence came full circle as Kareem walked toward me.

"As-salaam alaikum!" he announced. (The blessings of God be upon you!) And a blessing he was.

"Min fadlak!" I pleaded, pointing to my map in one hand while looking totally confused.

"Ada'tu tareeqi!" I said, even though it was self-evident I was lost.

Kareem was a young Syrian man whose Arabic name meant "noble one." It could have also meant "smiling one." When I pointed to the name of the place I sought on my map, he began to give me instructions. At step five or six, my eyes glazed over. Like the shepherd he must have been in his former life, Kareem then led me every step of the way to the front door of the Dar Halabia, my home sweet bayt in Aleppo.

As we walked toward Bab Antakia, Kareem began bashfully speaking in English. He had graduated college with a degree in engineering. "No work in Syria!" he remarked despondently, but he also expressed hope for the future. Before we parted, I offered him some Syrian pounds for his trouble, but he would have none it.

"Mister Guy," Kareem said, "you are a guest in my country!" He sounded as if he worked for the Syrian Tourist Agency.

"Alhamdulillah!" I said with a parting wave. (Praise be to God!) Thank you, Kareem, wherever you are.

Dar Halabia was a hotel, kind of, converted from a stone house built in the early eighteenth century. I knew I had to stay there because the brochure asserted that Dar Halabia's "12 rooms are visited regularly by the sun" and that the staff "endeavor hardly [sic] to make your holidays the happiest in our beautiful country, Syria." They triumphed on both counts, with exceptional success.

All grammar aside, I was minutes away from the stunning twelve-hundred-year-old Umayyad Mosque and the crown jewel of the region's antiquity known only as the Citadel. And Aleppo is as old as written history itself. Cuneiform tablets dating back to Mesopotamia some four thousand years ago record both the military and civil history of the region. Mesopotamia occupied the coveted location at the end of the Silk Route at one time. Half a millennium ago, Aleppo supplanted Damascus as Syria's most valuable trading metropolis.

Personally, I was enchanted by a little street café near my home. One afternoon I stopped for some Turkish coffee. I watched as two old gentlemen played backgammon while the TV overhead rolled

the titles to none other than *The Brady Bunch*. The world is laugh-
ingly mystifying at times.

One afternoon I went wandering down the Souk al-Atmah and
stumbled upon al-ShhBaa, a little shop selling handmade silver jewelry. While I was perusing some bracelets, the owner, Mohammed
Sazeb, came out.

"As-salaam alaikum!" he said, placing his hand over his heart.

"Wa alaikum salaam!" I replied with a similar gesture.

Mohammed then went off wandering through the richness of
the Arabic language while I stared blankly.

"Min fadlak!" I apologized. "Do you speak English?"

"La!" Mohammed declared, shaking his head no.

Then for no other reason than I had nothing to lose, I began to
search for another language. I had learned from living in Germany
that often when people meet, a common language is not a given. Most
Europeans I know speak at least four languages: Spanish, French,
Italian, and German. Even though I could read German and had
studied Spanish in high school and college, most recently I had lived
in Italy on and off for a number of years. I went with my long suit.

"Parla italiano?" I asked him.

"Si! Si! Certo! Io parlo italiano!" he said as his face widened into
a huge smile. (Yes! Yes! Of course! I speak Italian!)

And there you have it. In the grand, playful mystery of travel,
how unlikely was it that a half-Japanese, half-Italian visitor from
Honolulu would meet a Syrian silversmith in Aleppo and, in our
search to communicate, discover that we both spoke Italian?

In nothing short of a blink, I was led into his shop. Mohammed
called out to his wife for tea. We sat on the floor and I asked him, as
you might imagine, to begin at the beginning: why did a man from
Aleppo speak fluent Italian?

Mohammed recounted when he left Syria for Italy to learn the
art of the *agentiere*, the silversmith. He studied for twelve years in
Milan before coming home to start his business, get married, and
have children.

He was equally curious about me. I explained how my Italian-American father from Philadelphia (Pennsylvania, not Jordan) joined the US Army, was sent to Honolulu as an enlisted man, met my mother on Waikīkī Beach, got married, had five children, and that my parents had remained together for fifty-two years, until the day my father passed away. The army posted our family to Europe twice for nearly six years, and after graduate school I returned to live in Italy on and off for about seven more years.

We spoke for hours and ate cookies. His wife found the entire affair ridiculously entertaining, which it was. In the end, we exchanged mobile numbers. I purchased some jewelry for gifts and then set off to the Citadel museum.

Before I got there, I sat on a bench and gazed up at the majestic fortification near the city center.

"May I speak English with you?" a young woman wearing a hijab asked, waking me from my thoughts. She was pretty. I considered that as one of the greatest icebreakers ever.

"As-salaam alaikum!" I began. "Please do! I am happy to speak English with you."

"Thank you!" she said with an accent. "It is a rare treat to speak with a native English speaker," she added, bubbling with energy.

"I am Guy Sibilla" seemed like a good beginning. "May I ask your name, please?"

"Miss Kaukab Hashash," she said with a bright smile. "I am pleased to meet you!"

"How do you come to speak such wonderful English?" was what I wanted to ask, but instead, "How are you, Miss Hashash?" came out.

"Very well, thank you! I am with the Aleppo University English Department. I hope I am not bothering you," she offered politely. "I just could not miss the chance to try my English. We do not get many tourists in Aleppo."

If the truth be known, having just left Mohammed Sazeb and

his wife, I was up to here with tea. But sharing a cup of tea with Miss Hashash seemed to be the polite thing to do.

"May I buy you a cup of tea, Miss Hashash?" I offered.

"Wonderful!" she said happily. "If it is not too much trouble?"

"None whatsoever." I hadn't thought to ask my bladder.

We strolled off to a nearby café, where we sat and talked for some time. She was very progressive and clearly part of the new generation of young Syrians who wanted a more modern, secular society. She was thoughtful and very bright, and she reaffirmed my belief in the power of education.

As we departed, we exchanged mobile numbers and I asked her to send me a text message if she needed anything from the United States. I would be happy to send books, magazines, and whatever else that would pass the Syrian border inspectors.

By now, it was late evening as I wandered around Aleppo. The Citadel was beautifully lit at night, and the grand Umayyad Mosque was a cool oasis of calm and quiet from the streets. I stayed for a few days more, wandering the alleyways and museums until being lost in Aleppo occurred less often.

One afternoon, I decided I wanted to head out into the Syrian Desert. One of my well-traveled Milanese friends once told me that the best Roman architecture I could ever want to see was located in the Middle East. When an Italian says something like that to you, it is impossible not to take the idea seriously. This trip was, of course, proof that Laura was right.

In central Amman, I crawled all over the six-thousand-seat Roman amphitheater, which was built two thousand years ago when the city was called Philadelphia. On a plateau above Amman, I ambled through the remnants of the Temple of Hercules in the light of dawn after tiptoeing past the sleeping guards. In the heart of Damascus, the majestic ruins of the Temple of Jupiter at the night market become part historical site and part souk.

A fragment of history poked its tiny head up into the level of my active consciousness. Suddenly, there was the ancient city of

Palmyra, located deep within the Syrian Desert. In the third century CE, Zenobia, Queen of the East, ruled the Palmyrene Empire. The Romans ran head first into Zenobia's ambitions. Because of her, Palmyra almost didn't become Roman.

My modest ambition was to make the journey from a hot, crowded bus terminal in Aleppo to Homs, change buses, bypass the war in Iraq, and arrive unscathed in Palmyra—"Tadmor" if you are a traditionalist. I actually took a photo of the road sign that indicated Iraq was to the right and Tadmor was to the left. I watched to make sure our bus went *alyasar*.

After 180 kilometers or so, I passed through Homs, changed buses, and arrived finally at a place designated simply as "Tadmor" on my ticket. Pliny the Elder, a Roman writer and philosopher, reported on Palmyra twenty-two hundred years ago. Because of him, most maps still use the name Palmyra.

Exactly why my bus ticket read "Tadmor" and not "Palmyra" is anyone's guess. Some sources suggest that the former is related to the Semitic word *Tamar*, which refers to the fruit dates from the palms around the city. My recent experience with al-Hamra Hotel impressed upon me that names do matter. I'd be right in that case and wrong in this one. Whether I called it "Palmyra" or "Tadmor," or "Tadmur" for that matter, it was magnificent beyond description.

Palmyra was a physical manifestation of the abstract concept of power. When speaking of Palmyra two thousand years ago, consider the proposition that if Rome represents the highest achievements of humankind through its incomparable art, architecture, and politics, then Palmyra is the singular example of the Roman Empire's brute strength. Only Rome could declare that it would erect a glittering city of this size and magnitude in this dusty, desolate, unwelcoming place.

At one time there were over two hundred thousand inhabitants, many of whom were sustained with every luxury the Roman Empire could provide. Whatever was not available to the inhabitants of this bedouin outpost of the Silk Route through local production was packed, shipped, and caravanned into the sandy plains of Palmyra. Not to be ignored is the fact that all of this occurred in the middle of a vast wasteland where temperatures of 115°F in the shade are common.

I often wandered the barren sandy fields of Palmyra at 3:00 a.m. as shooting stars crisscrossed a jet-black night sky. There were no gates, no fences, no docents. Just me and the fallen stones of a collapsed empire.

Palmyra was intoxicating because it allowed me to do what Rome did not: touch the ancient. It was a powerful lesson on the transience of our own existence to hold a shard once turned by the hands of some Palmyrene potter two millennia ago, or to lean against a fallen stone column of a promenade along which once strolled beautiful women and their suitors, talking and laughing and thinking that the Palmyrene Empire would last forever.

The foolishness of such an idea is found in history books that have recorded the rise and fall of countless kingdoms. Even stones suffer their own mortality. One night while drifting through the scattered ruins of Roman columns, I jotted the following fragment of a poem into my journal:

> Oh Palmyra,
> we could not have loved you more
> and cared for you less,
> your Corinthian capitals
> lying sideways on the ground,
> proof that even stones
> have an end to their lives.

Several days earlier, my K. T. Pullman had pulled into the Tadmor bus station and my quest for a roof over my head resumed once again. Along the main street, shopkeepers displayed their wares on sidewalks. Men sat near doorways waiting for something, anything, to happen. Colorful fabric whipped in the wind. Dust devils rose and fell.

As tired as I was, through the fog my brain pulled up an arcane cinema reference to a movie in the late 1980s called *Ishtar*, in which Warren Beatty and Dustin Hoffman play lounge singers who head off to Morocco to improve their lot in life. The plot comes totally apart from there, so much so that *Ishtar* is considered to be one of the worst films ever made. Like, ever. Here are a few select films with which it shares such dubious distinction: *Santa Claus Conquers the Martians* (1964); *Bat Pussy* (1973); *Leonardo, Part 6* (1987); *Rancid Aluminium* (2000); and my favorite for worst film ever, *Catwoman* (2004).

With this as the questionable foundation of my decision about where I would sleep in Palmyra, I knew I was destined to stay at the Ishtar Hotel. Thus, in the late afternoon, I walked past a number of other hotels along Palmyra's main street and sauntered into the Ishtar Hotel, bemused by its namesake, the goddess of war and sexual love. My personal mantra was, "Make love, not war." Ishtar and I had some work to do.

No one was at the front desk. I did see a sign across the lobby that pointed downstairs to a bar called the Cave. I hoped it was a theme bar.

I stood around for a while until a tall, unshaven, soft-spoken man dressed in Western-style clothing came from around the corner behind the desk and asked me what I wanted.

"As-salaam alaikum!" I began as usual. "I would like a room, please!" I said, sounding hopeful.

"Okay," the old man uttered. He followed that with, "I don't work here."

I looked at him blankly, wondering, *Where do we go from here?*

"Write your name on this paper," he instructed. Then he added, "And have coffee until Maheer returns."

"Shukran!" I affirmed while scribbling away. "May I ask your name?" I inquired, extending my hand in greeting. "I am Guy."

"I am Adeeb al-Assad." He pronounced each word individually; his English was quite good. "I am bedouin guide."

"Great!" I exclaimed. "Maybe we can talk sometime about heading out into the desert for a few days? I would love to stay at a bedouin camp. And I would gladly pay you." I was sure the goddess Ishtar was smiling down on me.

"We have coffee now," Adeeb said.

"Okay then," I said, a little surprised, "now's good for me too." I followed Adeeb out the front door and turned left. Within about fifteen steps, we pulled up to a table set out onto the street just next to the curb. Clearly, Main Street was not a high-traffic zone. Adeeb ordered Turkish coffee. In short order, two cups were delivered.

"How long have you been a guide?" I asked, putting my toe into the water.

"I am guide and bedouin camping over twenty-five years," Adeeb replied while lighting a cigarette and looking at the horizon. "For me, in Palmyra is like jail," he declared. "Slowly, slowly, the life here is changing, and for me it no good. I am bedouin and I must be free." Then, almost as if he had forgotten, he asked me, "What country do you come?"

"I am from Hawaii," I answered. "Do you know this place?"

"I know pictures," Adeeb admitted. "You live in the water?"

"Next to water," I suggested for clarity. I wondered how I could explain our "water versus sand" realities. I guessed we were maybe a thousand kilometers from the sea, and goodness only knew how long it would take for us to get there from here. In the United States, we don't think of distance as space. We think of it as time. For instance, in Honolulu, we think of San Francisco as 5.5 hours, not 2,393 miles, away. In Palmyra, I sensed that distance was still measured in the number of days it might take to cross an expanse of sand.

"I think living in the middle of the ocean is a lot like living in this desert," I pronounced.

"How do you mean?" Adeeb asked, as if I had finally gotten his attention.

"Well, when you live on an island, you may be surrounded by

water, but you can't drink any of it because it is salt water. In that case, it might as well be sand. Don't you think so?" That came out a little more philosophical than I'd intended.

"And the ocean rises and falls like the dunes of the desert." I was reaching the end of the dimensions of my simile.

Adeeb looked at me curiously. "I think you are not like tourists who come here," he declared. "Tourists come from far away to look at old stone city and old stone tombs and old stone citadel. Only rocks. Then go!"

I wasn't quite sure where this was headed.

"You have rocks in your country, yes?" he concluded with a smirk.

"Yes! I have rocks in my country," I agreed, finally understanding his frustration.

I sipped my coffee, stifling the urge to confess that I had seen my fair share of rocks in my life. But Adeeb was right. Whether they are stones, buildings, or mountains, they are just stones, buildings, and mountains. As Mohan Chandran had suggested to me on one of my journeys across India, none of that can be exceptional unless, first, the people are special.

"Syria welcome all people!" Adeeb proclaimed, breaking my train of thought. "All foreigners. We share our culture with all!" he said with pride. "As Muslims, we respect all people. Jewish. Christian. They are welcome to Syria and in our homes."

I nodded my agreement.

"Maybe we can exchange our mobile numbers?" I showed Adeeb my Nokia. He looked surprised.

"I call Ishtar for your message," he said. "Maheer tell me. Is okay?"

"Shukran!"

We strolled back to the Ishtar Hotel, where we found that Maheer had returned.

"Mr. Guy! As-salaam alaikum! My uncle left note. Said you were for room?" he remarked cheerfully. He asked what room I wanted, as he had plenty. "You like quiet room in back?" he recommended helpfully.

I thought about it for a moment, and then I asked, "Do you happen to have a room overlooking Main Street?" I am not sure why this was preferable to me, but my wish was Maheer's command. Soon thereafter, I walked up a flight of stairs, opened my door, plopped my backpack onto the bed, and without breaking stride, moved to the window that opened up over the street. I stuck my head outside and, as I looked left and right, saw that I had a clear view up and down the street.

My choice turned out to be a good one. Several hours later, I was in my room drying off after a shower. As I wiped a towel over a wet head of hair, I heard a cacophony of car horns from downstairs. I walked over to the window and stuck my still wet head outside. A string of cars, pickup trucks, and jeeps were blaring their horns as part of a wedding celebration. It was infectious. Soon, I was clapping and whooping in support of the newlyweds as if I were late to the party.

The caravan of well-wishing family and friends lasted for maybe five minutes. It went quiet for a period, and then the whole noisy parade looped back down Main Street again. This happened five times.

The next morning, I met Adeeb for breakfast. We went next door where we had sat for coffee. Shortly a man drove up in a van. Unlike Adeeb, he was dressed in a *shalwar kameez*, the traditional long shirt and pants. He walked up to Adeeb, who rose to greet him. The men hugged, kissed each other's cheek once, and then kissed each other's left shoulder.

"As-salaam alaikum!" he said while turning in my direction and smiling broadly. He handed me his card, which read as follows:

Secure Tour Operator in Palmyra–Syria
Fuaz – Asad
Bedwen [*sic*] Man

[A camel was pictured here.]

I assumed Fuaz was a relative given that his last name was Asad. I ignored the fact that there was one less *s* in his name. Adeeb had decided we needed a driver; I guessed he chose to keep it all in the family.

When Adeeb sat down, he placed onto the table a well-worn copy of the *Helm Field Guide: Birds of the Middle East*. I had a momentary flashback to Botswana some years back when my guide, Baeti, pulled out *Sasol's Birds of Southern Africa* when we were on safari. It was a reflection of Baeti's love of the African environment within which he lived and worked, and his desire to understand it, preserve it, and monitor its change.

Adeeb, I was delighted to learn, apparently was cut from the same cloth. We ordered some roti and coffee and began smoking cigarettes. He confided that he'd had two agendas when he agreed to take me into the desert. First, he wanted to show me the life of the bedouin because he was happy to get out of the confines of Palmyra.

Second, since we were headed into the desert, he wanted to view the birdlife as part of his responsibility as a member of the Palmyra Society for the Protection of the Environment and Wildlife. Who knew? In scientific lingo, we were about to embark on a census of the *resident* as well as the *vagrant* birdlife of this barren region of the Syrian Arab Republic. I had liked Adeeb from the outset. This only served to prove that first impressions are almost always the right ones.

The following day, the three of us departed Palmyra. We began on a road, and then, somewhere, the road ended and we were just moving forward. I couldn't help but think that I'd been on this road before. I would begin to travel along a chosen route and then, without my even noticing, the path disappeared. I was wandering again. This time it was with Adeeb. We had set each other free.

In the course of several days with Adeeb and Fuaz, I saw my first flock of wild camels. I'd never imagined that such a thing was possible: to use the word *flock* and the word *camels* in the same sentence, I mean. The image of the wild camels was in and of itself astonishing. The significance of the absence of such an event ever before happening in my life was explained best by the fact that I had never been in a place where the opportunity to see wild camels ever had the chance to present itself.

That was a good life lesson: don't let fear keep you from taking chances, sometimes even with your life. Joy and wonder live there. In the words of an insightful American songwriter, Mary Chapin Carpenter, "I don't mind working without a net. I take my chances. I take my chances every chance I get."

While Fuaz, Adeeb, and I drove east into the desert, I didn't know if Adeeb had a plan. We did stop to buy bottles of water, which in and of itself seemed like a good plan. If Adeeb had a plan beyond that, it wasn't obvious. What was palpably clear, though, was the sandstorm we ran into early one afternoon.

Being on an island in the Pacific Ocean meant I lived with sand—benign white sand you rub your toes in and walk upon while strolling hand in hand with someone you love. This was not that sand.

In the hot summers of Italy, sirocco winds from the African Sahara would beat on us mercilessly, and we complained about it incessantly. But it was only hot dry air. In the Syrian Desert, a haboob is a "violent wind," as my Arab friends called it, the difference being that it is fast-moving hot air mixed with sand and dust. It is a force to be reckoned with.

Every couple of years, the Middle East gets pummeled by one of these storms that can grow so large as to encompass an area from Israel to Afghanistan. Today was one of those days.

Fuaz and Adeeb began speaking in concerning tones. Fuaz drove faster as the air began to get heavier and heavier. Adeeb pointed without using a compass for bearings.

Haboobs cause respiratory problems, gum up car engines, halt aircraft departures and landings, and basically make life stop in its tracks.

Finally, in the haze, we saw a bedouin tent. A few minutes later, we were all seated on rugs on the ground. Adeeb and Fuaz were unmistakably thanking this bedouin family for taking us in.

"Please thank them for me, Adeeb," I begged. "It is very kind of them to have us unannounced."

"This bedouin camp," Adeeb began, "they take us in as custom of our people. No one can be turned away from tent, because they know one day someone else somewhere else will take them in."

I had lived this custom before. I was on high glacial ice in the Karakoram Mountains of Pakistan. While at K2 Base Camp for nearly three months, I had fed and sheltered an assortment of Baltistani porters known to my cook and guide, Rozi Ali. In such frozen emptiness, no one was ever turned away.

After Adeeb said that, it seemed obvious. In Western cultures, we have learned to stay with strangers whose business it is to take us in. Hyatt. Marriott. Sheraton. Starwood. Holiday Inn. They and many other hotel chains have made their fortunes by not turning people away.

In Syria, an old land that is home to an ancient culture, cultural rules rule. Bedouin take in strangers, bedouin or not, knowing that one day it will be they who will need to rely upon the kindness of strangers to survive.

The tent scrambled as if we had appeared as part of a family reunion. The men came and brought smiling faces, cigarettes, and conversation. The women brought pots of tea, flatbread, hummus, sliced tomatoes, cucumbers, fried potatoes, onions, and dates. Soon it was evident that they knew and liked Adeeb.

I reached into my bag and pulled out a handful of candy for the children, who were curious but kept a safe distance. The oldest one looked toward one man, her father I presumed, who waved approval for her to receive my paltry gift. With that, she bounded fully into our area of the tent with the exuberance of every child you have ever seen run for candy.

She took the pile into her two tiny hands and ran toward the others. There was childlike screeching going on out of sight. The youngish-looking father tipped his head in my direction. Adeeb stretched out near the spread of food and politely reached in. It seemed we were going to be there a while. Just as we were getting settled in, the tent flap was thrown open and three men appeared.

"As-salaam alaikum!" one said. Western shirts, pants, and shoes. I looked at them and then looked at Adeeb. Then I thought of Khaled's warning that Syrian President Bashar al-Assad had many secret police whose job it was to make sure it was no secret they were the secret police.

"Wa alaikum salaam," the head of the family said. The men entered and sat down next to us around the food. More bread, tea, fruit, vegetables, and hummus appeared. Conversation continued for few hours until the wind stopped blowing and Adeeb gave me the nod that we were going.

I asked him quietly if I might leave some money for the family in thanks for their hospitality. They were not poor, but it seemed their good manners demanded some kind of reciprocation. In the reaches of my memory, I could hear my mother whispering, "The farther away you are from your home, the better you should behave."

"That would be well with them," he confirmed. So I did. And after many shukrans we were off.

"Who the hell were those guys?" I asked once we were back in the desert and away. It was somewhat rhetorical.

Fuaz kept his eyes on the road that wasn't there.

"They are the Assad people," Fuaz said without emotion. "They were in Palmyra."

Khaled had given me good advice.

Adeeb had not forgotten his bird survey responsibility for the Palmyra Society for the Protection of the Environment and Wildlife. "We go to falconer camp now? They catch for rich Saudi sheiks." That was not a question, by the way.

I'm guessing we kicked up sand and dust for another hour before Adeeb pointed to Fuaz.

"There!" Adeeb exclaimed. When we pulled up into camp, a

most distinguished-looking Arab man greeted us. He was tall, he sported an immaculately clean keffiyeh on his head, he was impeccably dressed, and he had the manners of a minister of government.

"As-salaam alaikum!" he said to Adeeb while using his open hand to indicate the entrance to his tent. He and his hunting partner camped out in the desert for months at a time using small mice attached to nearly invisible lines to attract wild falcons. When a falcon struck, a net collapsed on top of it.

We were soon seated on a rug and he was pouring from a pot of tea. Adeeb learned that they would stay encamped here throughout the falcon migration period hoping to catch a prize bird. For the right falcon, Saudi sheiks have been known to pay as much as a quarter of a million US dollars. Adeeb spoke with them for some time as they thumbed through different pages of his book of birds.

Meanwhile, I was thinking I could barely keep up with this day. We had run from a haboob into a bedouin camp. Then we left the not-so-secret secret police to come to a falconer's camp. This was already quite a day. It was also one that had to end, because Adeeb was to meet with some friends in Palmyra in a few days.

When at last I was back at the Ishtar, I thought to myself how fortunate it was that I had seen that awful movie with Warren Beatty and Dustin Hoffman. Because of that, I had chosen the Ishtar Hotel. Thank goodness Maheer was gone. And I was even more thankful that Adeeb had been there and offered to help as my guide.

In the years ahead, I know I will return to the region of the Tigris and Euphrates Rivers in whatever incarnation the lines in the sand may appear. It may sound self-evident, but political borders do not make a people. The next time I visit Damascus, I want to once again walk through Bab al-Salaam knowing that the Gate of Peace has resumed the splendor of humanity's greatest ideals.

FOR SOME TRAVEL MOJO

Voodoo needs a makeover.

In spite of all of its bad press, voodoo worship is so widespread that its followers out number those who ascribe to Jainism, Shinto, Bahai, Judaism and the next six smaller religious sects by a margin of over two-to-one.

Exploring the subject of voodoo intrigued me personally given the serious number of followers in various parts of the world. It has been quipped that Haitians are 85 percent Christian and 100 percent voodoo. All kidding aside, worship is a complex notion in some parts of our world.

Unlike Haiti, the tiny African nation of Benin has gone all-in. Voodoo has been decreed the official religion of the state, with Voodoo Day celebrated every January 10. Given Benin's commitment to voodoo, I knew a journey abroad was in my near future.

In June 2006 I wandered off to Africa without an assignment to write about where voodoo came from and what it was, and to show it some respect. I was supremely confident that I would find something interesting, and equally certain I could write one or two pieces that would a find a home somewhere. Sure enough, one of my editors in Jakarta, Indonesia, published my story entitled "Hands Off My Mojo!" It happened like the magic I was writing about.

Like most good stories, this one began to take real shape in Paris one night at a bar with a gin martini in the Charles de Gaulle Airport while waiting for Air France to fly me to Cotonou. There I met the tall, lovely, and colorfully dressed Tess. I was smitten. She was headed home. She did give me one bit of advice while we waited for our Air France departure. "Be careful in Cotonou," she declared with a mischievous laugh. "We are all thieves!"

Barely six hours after takeoff, I had arrived within one degree of being exactly on the opposite side of the planet from where I lived. Honolulu is –157 ° longitude, and Cotonou is +2° from the prime meridian. The difference between the Bight of Benin and Pearl Harbor is just about twelve thousand miles by my estimate, with a four-hundred-year time change.

Before I arrived in Cotonou, I knew voodoo existed closer to home. New Orleans has had a lengthy reputation for a thriving voodoo subculture. And the Caribbean Islands have had their own share of spells since the seventeenth-century slave ships arrived from Africa. Remarkably, the spiritual underpinnings of voodoo have not waned after all this time. Its believers remain as committed to their beliefs as vibrantly today as they have ever been.

Voodoo is also doing well in popular culture. Mostly we are indebted to Hollywood for keeping the light on voodoo with such movie malarkey as *Voodoo Woman*; *Voodoo Man*; *Voodoo Island*; or simply, and to the point, *Voodoo*. Even James Bond had a tangle with voodoo in the mercifully forgettable *Live and Let Die*.

I haven't even touched upon the zombie movie genre.

But let me suggest a yummier alternative. There is Voodoo Doughnut of Portland, Oregon, which has pastries so delightful that you can't help being possessed by them. It's a sugar curse.

That solitary fact about Benin and Voodoo Day drove my decision to head to the region of Africa once designated exotically as Afrique Occidentale Française. Just a century ago, the major European colonizing nations divided up Africa as if they were cutting a cake. The freedom to colonize a landmass with seemingly limitless natural resources and diversity was irresistible. All of Europe and South America could fit inside the boundaries of the African continent and have another two million square miles to spare. Over fifteen hundred different tribes, each with their own language, live and thrive in Africa.

With fierce determination, France, Great Britain, Germany, Italy, Portugal, Spain, Belgium, and others staked their claims. But that was the past. As of today, there are fifty-four nation-states in Africa. When I advised one of my editors that I was headed to the land where voodoo began, he gleefully wrote the following in a sidebar:

> Every so often our contributing editor Guy Sibilla gets himself into some tight spots. This month he finds himself in "deep voodoo" in Lomé, Togo, home of the spirit worship brought to the New World via seventeenth-century slave ships. He found it especially poetic that as a Buddhist, he could stand in the shadow of Lomé's Christian Cathédrale du Sacré Coeur while Muslims greeted one another and patient voodoo chiefs sat at the Marché des Fétiches ten minutes away to conjure up the power of African magic.

The Hotel du Lac in Cotonou was home for the next several weeks. There I met Christian, one of the front desk managers. I reposed a fair level of trust and confidence in his opinions given his knowledge of Nigeria and the endorsement of the hotel manager.

I confided in Christian that I was in search of a voodoo chief for my story. I told him of my plans to go to Nigeria as a good place to conduct some research and said that I already had a visa. He did not try to reassure me.

"Everything they say about Nigeria is true, Mr. Guy," which sounded supportive until, "but sometimes it is not." I confess that when Christian gave me this advice, I had no clue what he was trying to say.

Even Hassan, one of the administrative staff whose Yoruba people come from Nigeria, cautioned me against traveling into Nigeria alone. It would be, in his words, "a nightmare" given the value of my cameras and my US passport.

Between Christian's fear, Hassan's words of concern, and Tess's warning of rampant thievery, I did what any savvy traveler would do who was smart enough not to want to tempt fate: I changed directions.

"Maybe it is better to find a voodoo chief not in Nigeria?" I said, recognizing Christian's delicate attempt to dissuade me. "What about Togo?" I asked.

"This is better idea," Christian said, clearly happy that I had decided to go west from Cotonou to Togo instead of east to Nigeria. "Lomé is dangerous," he observed, "but not as dangerous as Nigeria!" Christian continued not to reassure me.

What Christian had neglected to warn me was that the bush taxi drive from Gare de Jonquet to Togo might have been as dangerous as Nigeria itself. The process for grabbing a ride to Lomé was easy. Since I wanted to go west, I went to the bush taxi stand in the western part of Cotonou and bought a seat in a Peugeot 505 headed my way.

This was merely one legacy of the French in this region: the Peugeot. We slanged them as "Cinq-Sans-Cinqs"—505's. For about 3,000 CFAs, or about US$6, I bought a seat to Lomé. A CFA, pronounced "see-fa," is French currency issued by the Banque Centrale États de L'Afrique de L'Ouest.

Getting that seat is a story in and of itself. From the street fronting my hotel, I jumped onto the backseat of a *zémidjan*, a two-wheeled, death-by-motorcycle ride to Gare de Jonquet. Zémidjans are operated by young men who drive them like they are immortal. It is fun and harrowing at the same time, but amusing only after you arrive without incident.

As I jumped off the back of the zémidjan at Gare de Jonquet, a bunch of young touts each tried to pull me to their waiting drivers. I held them at bay with some candy as I scanned the cars for someone who looked calm. I knew that even after I paid for my seat, I had to wait until the other three seats of the Cinq-Sans-Cinq were sold before I could depart. So I looked for a car with three people standing around it. Upon finding one, I ran over to give that driver my CFAs, and off we all went.

In an hour or so we arrived at the nastiest, dirtiest, most un-wholesome border crossing I had ever seen. Hilla-Condji is the *fron-tière* between Benin and Togo. The part that made this dangerous was the amount of unregulated flammables crossing the border. Hilla-Condji seemed to be an entry point for illegal gasoline being brought into Togo via Benin from Nigeria. They call this gasoline *essence*. It was *contrebande*. And it was everywhere.

I completed some paperwork and submitted it with a *dash*, a gift of CFAs to the official reviewing my paperwork. I thought of it as a kind of rush fee. After someone somewhere accepted my dash, I got my visa and sped off toward Lomé.

Understandably, few outside of Africa have ever heard of Togo, and even fewer can name its capital city. With barely eight hundred thousand people, Lomé is the country's seat of government, industrial center, and chief port. From here, Togo exports coffee, cocoa, cotton, and a modest amount of refined oil. It also exports voodoo.

Do not make the mistake of equating size with power. Togo is a tiny sliver of land of 22,000 square miles. It is .002 the size of the entire African continent. But after a few days here, I realized Lomé was so spiritually powerful that its influence extended across 5,354 miles (give or take) of Atlantic Ocean.

At the same time, I learned that voodoo really isn't such scary stuff. The word means, quite literally, "spirit" in the several lan-guages found along the West African coastline. There are spirits and potions conjured for healing and for helping with every kind of problem from forgetfulness to erectile dysfunction. To just about everyone else in the world, voodoo means blood rituals, zombie possession, and dolls punctured with pins.

These kinds of revelations are what make traveling fun and, to my mind, necessary. I came here with my misguided preconceptions, thinking scourges and the walking dead would dominate my story. By the end of my trip, I had instead discovered a cure to help me get my groove back for those times when it went south.

I met Ayuite while wandering through the main Marché de Féticheurs in Lomé. He spoke good English and said he would help me for a modest charge. I was in no position to refuse.

He told me, "Voodoo is strong medicine!"

I agreed that it was certainly as strong as the odor of rancid animal flesh roasting under the dry equatorial sun. In one 360-degree sweep by my eyes, I saw that the pageant of death within which I stood included the heads and sometimes the bodies of crocodiles, hyenas, wild dogs, cobras, vipers, lizards, monkeys, zebras, fruit bats, parrots, gazelles, and a bunch of wildlife whose identity stretched beyond my paltry knowledge of zoology. Mixing these animal parts with the right herbs and incantations, voodoo chiefs channel the forces from the other side to our side. As a result, some people are possessed, others are cursed, and some are healed. It is all voodoo.

I was knee-deep in wildlife, or what used to be wildlife. In the Marché de Féticheurs, this was the storehouse for the apothecary. Before you judge, you need to know that this is an ancient healing art. Medicine men like the voodoo chief I sought in Lomé are referenced in Islamic texts found in Baghdad in the eighth century CE and even Islamic Spain three hundred years later.

Closer to home, I could walk into Chinatown in Honolulu and disturb some wrinkled dude who spoke Cantonese sitting behind a wall of three hundred drawers to mix up some powder of lizard parts, berries, and herbs to cure what ailed me. My point is that there are natural healers closer to me (and probably you) than Africa.

"Voodoo chief there," Ayuite said, pointing to the doorway of a small hut after we had walked some distance through the ingredients used for conjuring mojo. He entered first and I followed, ducking under a stunted wooden door cut into a mud-walled hut.

It was sweleteringly hot—much hotter than outside and a bit more smelly—and downright eerie.

There were no windows, and consequently there was no breeze. The floor was hard-packed dirt. No table. No chairs. But there was Chief Guendon, who sat on a small wooden stool in the middle of the room.

Ayuite spoke for a while. Perhaps they were discussing how their families were, or whose daughter was pregnant, or what Togo's chances were for advancing in this year's World Cup football tournament. I don't know. But eventually, Ayuite turned to me and asked, "Chief asks for what you want?"

Now that was a really great question. I considered that I was in the presence of a voodoo chief who, for a price, was prepared to do whatever I asked. This was like finding a lamp in a souk in Amman with a genie inside. Did I have an axe to grind? Was I greedy? Maybe there was a Nobel Prize in Literature in my voodoo future? Not.

I began to think that if I bought something, it would humor Chief Guendon. Perhaps it would even make him smile. If I didn't buy something, I was afraid it would be like making my father angry, except worse.

I could feel my karma calling. Then, remembering who and what I was, I asked Ayuite to ask Chief Guendon for some travel mojo to keep me safe. Ayuite passed on my request as a conversation ensued. Then Chief Guendon began rummaging through a small pile of amulets. Satisfied with one in particular, he held it between his palms, recited something under his breath, and exhaled on the object slowly.

After a few moments, he handed me a wooden stick with a tiny hole in it. I was instructed to speak into the opening while asking for safe passage. When my request was complete, I was to plug the hole with another little piece of wood to keep the mojo inside until I reached my destination.

Chief Guendon asked me do this in front of him to make sure I understood.

"Please get me out of here and back to my room in Lomé safely," I whispered inaudibly into the tiny hole. Then I stuck the piece of wood into the hole and dropped the stick into the cargo pocket of my khaki pants. And that's how I got my travel mojo in Afrique Occidentale Française.

The next moment, I watched as the chief cupped four small cowrie shells in his hands and threw them onto the dirt floor at his feet. "Chief says mojo costs for 5,000 CFAs," said Ayuite while staring at the ground. His voice reminded me of Darth Vader without the heavy breathing. The West African franc used in this region has its value tied to the French franc. Black market moneychangers will give you approximately 500 CFAs to US$1 depending on the day, their mood, and your negotiating skills.

Throughout all of this, I had been sitting quietly on a tiny, uncomfortable wooden stool. My butt hurt. Perhaps that pain in my derrière set me off. My discomfort manifested itself into some kind of twisted semblance of courage. "I think five thousand CFAs [roughly US$10] is too much," I said calmly, surprising even myself.

All travelers know that distance in terms of time and space often provides an illuminating perspective. What seems rational at the time appears absurd, and perhaps offensive, back at home, like negotiating a price for my travel mojo, for instance. Imagine sitting across from a voodoo chief and haggling about cost! What if he had been offended at my kibitzing over price? I might have awakened, if at all, the following morning with a severe rash or no teeth—or worse. And all for the sake of saving a few bucks.

But I had good reason, if not a sound mind. In the République Togolaise, as it is across most all of French West Africa, the daily wage hovers at roughly US$3 per day. I wasn't trying to be cheap. It was only the fact Chief Guendon was asking me to pay a half a week's wages for my mojo, the efficacy of which, I might add, remained unproven. That just didn't seem fair. Back then. Now in my world of Western wages, telling a man believed by most everyone in

Lomé to have magical, mystical, and supernatural powers to lower his price seems utterly silly, if not spiritually reckless altogether.

Without as much as a harrumph, Chief Guendon gathered up the shells and cast them once again onto the dirt before his feet. I heard more words that sounded similar to the dialogue from the Mos Eisley Cantina in the first *Star Wars* film. Then, Ayuite turned to me and informed me that the amulet for my travel mojo had been reduced to 4,000 CFAs. The spirits were being kind.

This brought me to a very nonspiritual observation: everything in Africa is negotiable. The cost of an item depends on what the seller is willing to accept and what the buyer is willing to pay. I'm guessing, but I don't think Chief Guendon took offense. So far I remain healthy and still have all of my teeth.

Ayuite interrupted my daydreaming. "Chief asks if you want other mojo," he asked.

"Like what?" I wondered.

Like anything and everything I learned. Got a cold? Off-key in karaoke? Allergies bothering you? Chief Guendon's got voodoo for you, but none of it will be covered by your health-care plan. Trust me on this.

Ayuite explained that football players regularly visited for a drink of an extract of starfish or elephant bones for strength.

Chief Guendon said he also used resources from Africa's elephant. Then he showed me some plants he had retrieved. I recalled my guide Baeti Samotanzi in Botswana telling me the same thing.

"We use elephant dung to heal people," Baeti had told me. One day I found a long trail of bowling-ball-size dung and went over and took a photograph of it. Baeti looked at the huge balls of poop laying there and commented, "Elephant travel long distance, and so they carry plants long way in their stomachs."

While on safari in Botswana, I had educated myself on African wildlife by reading portions of a classic treatise on the big game of the sub-Saharan plains. *Smither's Mammals of Southern Africa: A Field Guide* is written in the kind of English that makes me feel like English is my second language. For instance, Smither describes the African elephant at page 130 as "Enormous and unmistakable." Only an Englishman could describe a ten-thousand-pound elephant in three words, including the conjunction.

Elly, as Baeti affectionately called them, eat more than three hundred pounds of roughage daily and produce two hundred pounds of detritus. African voodoo doctors like Chief Guendon would pick through the piles of dung, take undigested plants from faraway places, and use them locally as cures. Scatology meets pharmacology.

Okay. Enough of that shit.

Chief Guendon told Ayuite that people came to him complaining that their good spirits had left them. The cure for this was a concoction of vulture or owl mixed with a reasonable amount of blood, usually the blood of the person seeking the relief. The chief instructed his charge to put the liquid in strategic places around his or her home so the spirits would return in short order.

Chief Guendon won't let your asthma slow you down. If you drink his mixture of tortoise shell powder, an herbal concoction, and some honey with water, you can join the track team.

Ayuite explained that if you can't recall where you put your keys, or anything else for that matter, Chief Guendon can prepare a powder made from monkey, gorilla, or chimpanzee. If he adds selected herbs and water, then you will end up with a goop that will ensure you don't forget a thing, especially the taste.

Singers who need help with their pipes bathe in a preparation of African parrot powder. Chief Guendon guarantees every note.

Last but not least, Ayuite said, "This one much popular!" Chief Guendon pointed to the rows and rows of bats at his feet. I was told to take the ash of a burned fruit bat, add selected herbs, and mix it with alcohol. I wasn't told how much alcohol goes into the formula. I was simply told that imbibing liberal amounts seemed to work better. An hour or so after drinking the sludge, the voodoo would kick in.

"You make sex all the night, and your partner very happy!" He flexed his forearm and pointed it toward the heavens for emphasis.

I gave him the I-get-the-picture wink.

"It true!" Chief Guendon protested, even though my inner voice had its doubts. I thought of Pfizer and all of those tiny blue pills. The chief didn't realize I was smiling because he had confirmed what I already knew was true: the farther away you travel, the more you recognize home. Notwithstanding language, culture, religion, and food, travel is the process of walking forward until the place you left appears right in front of you.

Thus, armed with forces far greater than those any mere mortal should possess, I left Togo with the knowledge that I was prepared for whatever the world could throw at me. While I don't think of myself as particularly superstitious, I need to report that I did in fact return from Africa unscathed.

Coincidence, or cause and effect?

Whatever.

But I am taking my travel mojo with me from here on out. And if you need any help with what ails you, ask your health-care provider if Chief Guendon is covered under your plan.

WATCHING WHO CROSSED
THE HONDO

Welcome to the jungle.

My compadres in the boat, Cathy, David, Sarah, and Ruth, were all students attending the University of Texas–San Antonio (UTSA) Summer Field School in 2005. They were studying anthropology or one of its many subdisciplines as part of their degree curriculum. I was old enough to have fathered any one of them (or all of them for that matter). As I am known to do, I arrived in Belize without knowing anyone, not even the friend of a friend without whom I wouldn't be sitting on this modest boat on a skinny creek separating Belize from Mexico.

One of my dear friends, Miriam, a professor of linguistics at the University of Hawaii, had sent a letter of introduction to her colleague Laura who taught anthropology at the University of Texas. My letter of credentials followed with a donation to the research project. Suddenly, but clearly not miraculously, I had a position on Laura's team.

For a couple of months, I would live in a Central American jungle to write a story on the research being undertaken on pre-Colombian Maya civilization at the Programme for Belize Archaeological Project (PBAP). I already had an assignment from a newspaper and a magazine. I can't explain it, but it seemed that stories on the Middle East, ancient Rome, and the disappeared Maya civilization always found a home.

The first thing Laura sent to me was a reading list that looked a lot like a freshman course syllabus. A visit to Amazon.com and a credit card charge later, I had, just that precipitously, built a small section on my bookshelf specializing in a subject area about which I knew nearly nothing: the Maya.

This is a terrific illustration of an easily overlooked rule of writing: not all writing is writing. As a journalist, sometimes you get lucky and you meet the right editor at the right time in your career. I did. As he used to pound into my pointy little head, "Writing is *not* writing; writing is *rewriting*!" True that.

The corollary to the aforementioned rule is, "Writing is not *just* writing; writing is *reading*!" This is especially true for travel writers. For a country to be interesting as you wander aimlessly across its geography, munch through its menus, stare at its architecture, tap your feet to its music, or whatever, you need to read to prepare the fertile open spaces in your brain waiting to be plowed and planted with knowledge.

Sometimes I find I am reading much more than I am writing. One of my favorite sources for understanding a country or a culture, or even a continent, is an anthology of poetry from that place. I don't know why it affects me so profoundly, but poetry is writing where every single word is loaded with meaning. It is the poet's desperation to express longing, grief, ecstasy, pleasure (or pick an emotion) with brevity that makes a poem so powerful. Poetry captures, in my opinion, the heart of a place. Try it. You will thank me later.

After we snaked our way down to the water's edge, two poorly dressed Belize border guards and a nonseaworthy-looking rowboat greeted us. This outpost of jungle immigration and customs did not require paperwork for us to cross into Mexico unless that paper looked a lot like Belizean dollar bills. The five of us passed cash to the guards to emigrate, and soon enough we were crossing the Río Hondo on a wobbly boat, moving from Belize to the land of Mexican tequila.

"Does that sign say, 'Welcome to La Unión'?" someone behind me commented.

"Yeah!" I confirmed. "And I bet the other side says, 'Thank you for visiting La Unión'! This looks like one small-ass town."

Anthropology summer camp included a lot of wearisome work. For the last few weeks we had been trudging through dense jungle conducting surveys to locate Maya structures. Since we had completed a few weeks of challenging plodding, we all earned a play day. One afternoon, we grabbed one of the camp trucks and headed for the Mexican border. Summer school in Belize was, after all, summer school in a foreign country, and that meant taking some time to engage in friendly foreign relations.

After crossing the Hondo, we walked down La Unión's main street until we ran into a place called the Aurelia for some food and drink. I'm not judging, but if you are going to name your place something akin to "the Golden One," then you really should strive to be more presentable than just a bar-slash-restaurant. Then again, after being in the bush for a month and after the five of us kept repeating those three magic words, "Cervezas, por favor!", all of a sudden *we were golden.*

While still sober, I remembered seeing rows of shops whose storefronts spilled onto the sidewalk. At a glance I could see inventory like soap, aluminum pots, hard liquor, cheap dishes, T-shirts, towels, candy, plastic cups, canned goods, hammers, bandannas, light bulbs, batteries, rope, electrical wire, toilet paper, razor blades, toothpaste, Bic ballpoint pens, chicken fencing, and I think a piñata—all in the same tiny store. Residents sat at tables along the road in front of restaurants whiling away the time by watching who crossed the Hondo. It was hot as hell, and the cold beers were just what the doctor ordered. That and grilled chicken tacos.

I don't remember if we ever got into the Mexican tequila. Perhaps we did, which would explain why my notes were a little fuzzy. At some point in time, we all strolled back down Main Street arm in arm, talking and laughing about nothing and everything and pleased that we were all here together, safe, happy, and doing good work.

Back in Belize we couldn't be more content. We were full of good Mexican home cooking, cervezas, and maybe tequila. I can't remember much beyond having the sensation that joyous moments in life rarely got much better.

The next morning I woke up with a red bandanna wrapped around my neck. I surmised that was my La Unión souvenir. My group met up at the dining hall a little later than usual for breakfast, looking a little rough around the edges. Today we were headed back out into the jungle for more surveying.

Because of their years of work in Belize, UTSA had been granted rights to construct a permanent camp within the Maya Biosphere Reserve. The PBAP was conducted within a preserve consisting of roughly 250,000 acres open only to scientists conducting approved research. Over the centuries, tomb raiders have done irreparable damage to countless Maya sites across Central America in search of artifacts to sell on the black market.

Our small band of researchers and scholars couldn't begin to undo the damage that had already been done to many Maya settlements. If digging into ancient structures for valuables to sell was the difference between feeding your family and having them go hungry, who knows what choices each of us would make. But the damage meant that we were in a race against time to find undiscovered sites before the tomb raiders got there.

The evidence of the pillaging was obvious. Huge "robber trenches" gutted the temple mounds right through their centers. Sometimes we felt that our effort to find and preserve unknown ancient Maya sites was futile, even hopeless. Mahatma Gandhi did offer us some consolation when he suggested that perseverance was in and of itself the reward: "Whatever you do will be insignificant, but it is very important that you do it."

After landing in Belize City, a couple of Texas undergrads and I were soon being jolted about in a red beaten-up pickup truck en route to the place of our insignificance. Because of the PBAP's scientific importance, this protected zone was an annual summer home to cultural anthropologists, archaeologists, and biologists, as well as botanists, geologists, entomologists, herpetologists, environmentalists, historians, astronomers, and journalists like me. Belize, Mexico, and Guatemala determined that the Maya Biosphere Reserve was so worthy of protection that they entered into an international treaty recognizing the PBAP across their sovereign boundaries.

Although our encampment was stuffed with some of the most educated people in the world, the infrastructure needed some engineering. The main PBAP research center was a mix of six modest wooden structures with bunks for sleeping, a covered camp area for tents, a lab for teaching as well as sifting through pottery shards, and a mess hall.

In one of the hottest jungles on earth, however, the PBAP didn't have a shower. So we built one. If you squinted your eyes really tightly, you'd determine that the wooden tower structure ten meters tall vaguely resembled what a rustic Central American small-scale copy of the Eiffel Tower would look like.

One day the entire camp was rallied to hoist a huge fiberglass tank to the top of the tower. The empty container was rolled through camp and set at the base of the frame. Ropes were tied around the tank and draped over the top of the tower. The camp formed a line on the opposite side. With rope in hand and without the help of any structural engineers from whom help would have been gladly accepted, the PBAP prepared to engage in a tug-of-war, with the tank and the force of gravity on one side and sheer force of will on the other.

As the group of twenty or so optimistic students enthusiastically yanked on the line, the tank inched its way up the side of the tower. Breathlessly we towed the line like we were *Rapa Nui* moving a fifteen-ton stone *moai*. Even though I was surrounded by brilliant scientists, it was apparent to me that many were only marginally familiar with the laws of the physical universe. I deduced this from the simplistic solution to getting the big thing on the ground to the top of the other big, vertical thing: apply brute strength in the face of arcane laws of physics like coefficients of friction, tensile strength of rope, and load-bearing ratios of construction materials. My younger brother, Vic, is a licensed engineer. I imagined him standing beside me, slowly shaking his head back and forth in silent disbelief, if not altogether disapproval.

Long story short, optimism prevailed. At the end of the day the PBAP had a gravity-driven, cold-to-the-bone shower. At the same time, I now had a memory to refer to as proof that at least on one occasion, perseverance had triumphed over adversity.

Unlike the heights of the shower tower, the latrine was low-tech and thankfully away. A flush consisted of a scoop of lime powder. The UTSA team had arrived a little earlier in the summer than other student programs, but the growing stalagmite of human feces had already begun to reach unpleasant heights. By the way, one of the tasks of latrine duty was to topple the tower of shit with a big stick. I'm not kidding.

Laura was the professor in charge of our group. She had made our introductions at our first gathering in the mess hall. She specialized in characterizing ancient Maya architecture. By studying the locations of residential and lesser temple structures, she could then study how land, labor, and institutional memberships converged to create the highly complex community we know as the Maya Empire. Laura was brilliant and her work difficult.

She told us, in the parlance of anthropology, that we were going to be "surveyors." Our job was to head out daily into portions of the jungle that had never been mapped before and record what we found. The historical implications on the ecology, the number of residents sustained in the area, the size of satellite political, social, and economic units, and the size of regional seats of governance would all be discerned from the new data we were to wrench from the jungle.

In the lab, we were introduced to our survey equipment. Orientation included working the Bruntons, our handheld transits for taking GPS coordinates and dividing ourselves into two teams. Both teams had a lead person to shoot degree bearings, hack through dense prickly brush with a machete, and pull a tape measure every twenty-five meters. A second person was to anchor the tape and assist in ensuring the course was true. The third member was to record the coordinates and any scientifically significant structures.

It wasn't as easy as it sounds.

I wasn't blaming the bush. I'd been in and out of a few jungles in my time. Borneo. Papua New Guinea. Ghana. Botswana. Zambia. And others. This jungle, though, had teeth.

As you might expect of an equatorial wilderness, it was an unmercifully hot, damp, moist place. As far as I could discern in my short time here, there were only two types of weather in Belize: rain and threatening rain. When it did rain, it was that relentless, pounding, soaking, vengeful torrent I knew so well from other rain forests.

When it was threatening rain, just enough sunlight would peek through the canopy to ensure the *húmedo* hovered at 100 percent. Dry clothes always felt damp. Wet clothes never dried. The inescapable moisture ruined or rotted everything, including cotton shirts, socks, and pants.

If my father were alive, I am confident he would have said that times like these build character. Honestly, I thought I already had enough character. One anthropologist put a finer point on it by sporting a T-shirt that read, "The Strong Survey – The Rest Excavate." I didn't get that when I first arrived at the PBAP, but after a few weeks of hacking jungle surveys, I caught his vibe.

The joy of being constantly wet was enriched by the ever-present threat of infections. Insect bites caused infections, and there was plenty of opportunity for being bitten considering the array of fleas, ticks, brown recluse spiders, tarantulas, mosquitoes, botflies, fruit bats, ants, beetles, and every other crawly creature entomologists studied while they were feeding on us surveyors.

One night at camp I walked over to the latrine and entered the tented area. As protocol required, I picked up a stick and banged on the wooden seat and around the hole before I sat down to chase away the spiders that liked to call that place home. While I waited patiently for nature to take its course, I looked down as my head-lamp tracked the movement of the plumpest example of a tarantula I had ever seen—with my pants down at my knees.

When I described it in a story, I wrote that it appeared to be "roughly the size of a moped." Quite motivated at that point, I scooped some lime and gingerly got out of there. As I was leaving, I walked past a young, pretty undergrad from another research group who was waiting in line.

"Be sure to bang on the box," I warned with controlled alarm. "There's a spider in there." I held the tent flap open as she walked by, giving me a "Really?" look as she closed the canvas behind her.

I strolled back to camp smug that I had been morally forthright.

"Hey, what's so funny?" Sarah asked me when I returned to the group, who were sitting under the stars.

"Wait for it," I said. With that, a scream taken from the soundtrack of *The Texas Chainsaw Massacre* came from the direction of the latrine. I explained to my fellow surveyors what I had seen in the latrine and what I had said to warn the unsuspecting undergrad.

"Technically, we call them arachnids," Cathy noted, laughing.

If the bugs and arachnids didn't present enough ways to get sick, then there were the thorns. The poetically named *bayal* vines are a wispy green growth covered with thousands of thorns of hypodermic-needle-like sharpness. If you inadvertently caught a loose end on your clothing and kept walking, the remainder of the vine would build tensile energy like a stretched rubber band. Unless you backed up slowly, the vine could snap and send an array of thorns into your soft flesh like a series of machine gun bullets across a wall.

Then there were the snakes. This jungle had lots and lots of snakes. These were not serpents in the Shakespearean sense of that word: "O serpent heart with a flowering face!" The assorted Central American snakes were far less amorous. They were prepared to envenom any one of us surveyors with a dose of a neurotoxin or hemotoxin at a moment's misplaced footfall. It was Disneyland for herpetologists.

I had prepared myself before I left home with a morbid inventory of death-by-snakebite scenarios. It began with the Maya coral snake, which has one of the deadliest neurotoxic venoms on earth.

As frightening as that sounded, I had a personal aversion to the *fer-de-lance*. One snake expert in camp described this member of the pit viper family as grumpy. I don't want to get off on a rant here, but I happen to use that adjective to describe myself in the morning before I have had a cup of coffee. No one dies, though, if someone surprises me, say, in the kitchen.

I did in fact meet a fer-de-lance early one morning in camp. I awoke, grabbed my toothbrush, and walked a few steps from my bunk to brush my teeth in the cool green halo of dawn. Just as I went to spit a mouthful of saliva mixed with Crest, a few feet away a viper *this big* slithered out from under some leaf litter and stared at me with that grumpy sort of look. I took the hint and slithered back to my bunk.

Then there was the neotropical rattlesnake. Enough said.

To round out the rest of the crew, there were pit vipers like the Mexican moccasin, the jumping viper, the hognose viper, and the eyelash viper.

The good news was that most of these snakes hunted at night when their infrared-sensing zones made them unmatched killing machines when it came to other animals walking around with the false belief that the cover of darkness protected them. The bad news was this group of nastiness hid in the shadows of fallen trees and leaf litter that we, as surveyors, traipsed across all day long.

As scary as that sounds, I had dealt with this situation before. I was once in Puebla, several Mexican states away to the northwest, climbing Popocatépetl (17,887 feet). The approach to base camp was by horseback, and then on foot through the Mexican bush.

There was also the time the president of Guatemala choppered into a jungle LZ and met me on my birthday. That deserves some explanation.

El Presidente de la República de Guatemala Oscar Berger dropped out of a cloudless blue Central American sky in a Sikorsky VH-3D. His landing zone was a patch of dry turf otherwise surrounded by boggy lowlands adjacent to tiny Carmelita.

With military efficiency, a platoon of humorless-looking men equipped with Israeli Galil SAR carbines deployed in a measured radius from the drop-off point. It was a menacing circle of presidential forces sporting fully laden Blackhawk tactical vests.

Until Oscar showed up, everything had been fairly calm and quiet except for the jackasses, the two of which objected vociferously to being strapped down with bundles of food and water as we prepared to depart for the interior. Of all the things I had tried to anticipate while organizing a trek to El Mirador, the spectacle of this presidential firepower did not make that list.

While surrounded by mule drivers, docile husbands, startled mothers, curious shopkeepers, and a half dozen or so marginally clothed children, I turned to Geronimo Romero, one of the Maya guides, and gave him a "Can you believe this?" look. No one had any way of knowing that today, the president of Guatemala would decide to come personally to thank Richard Hansen of Idaho State University and his a team of scientists for their six months of research in the Central American jungle.

Evidently, someone considered this an important photo op. That was the unpredictable and most unlikely of circumstances that brought Carmelita, el presidente de la República de Guatemala, and me together on January 16 for my birthday.

After the chopper landed, I reached down, unzipped a pocket of my backpack, and grabbed my cameras. I rushed toward the men in black with my press pass in hand, elevating it above my head. The nearest armed security guard waved me through.

"Buenos días, Señor Presidente!" I blurted out, embarrassed by my Spanish. President Oscar Berger looked genuinely startled at my greeting. Perhaps it was my poor pronunciation. Maybe he was mulling over why an American journalist would come this far to cover what he believed to be a local event.

I declared shamelessly to el presidente that today was my birthday.

"Feliz cumpleaños!" the president of Guatemala said, shaking my hand before marching off to the tent erected for his press conference.

"Gracias, Oscar! Tenga una buena día!" I shouted as Oscar walked away, thanking him and bidding him a good day. Sadly, after I expressed my thanks to the president, that was the last time we ever spoke. Politicians.

With each passing day at PBAP, I began to understand more and more about life in the ancient Maya world. When you are surrounded by such intelligence, you can't help but learn things just by sitting and listening to the conversations while eating breakfast and, if we weren't in the field, lunch. It sounds self-evident, but intelligent people tend to have clever conversations. These just happened to take place in a sweaty jungle instead of the student union center.

My reading list included a delightful primer on the Maya civilization called simply *The Maya*, by Michael D. Coe. It began at the beginning, with the Maya creation myth.

Before there was recorded time, the Maya creator, Itzamná, gave this land to the Maya. In an act of inexplicable penury, Itzamná provided the Maya with terrain largely devoid of natural lakes or streams.

Consequently, priests with a penchant for meteorology learned to predict the seasons of rain and drought out of necessity. In turn, they employed the indispensable ingenuity of engineers who designed and constructed a catchment system for storing water. By effectively managing life-sustaining water, the Maya civilization, anthropologists estimated, may have numbered nearly two million people at its apex.

The Maya culture flourished for thousands of years before Christopher Columbus stumbled accidentally onto the New World. The scent of riches in gold, silver, and precious stones propelled Spain to finance expeditions from Europe to where I was sitting.

The inception of colonial occupation fell upon the willing shoulders of Hernán Cortés de Monroy y Pizarro and his conquistadors. Cortés brought his Spanish flag and a marauding force. This spelled the beginning of the end for the Maya. In gratitude for Cortés's service to the crown, the Spanish king conferred upon his loyal servant the noble title of Marqués del Valle de Oaxaca for the gift of the New World territory and its riches.

Besides unwanted subjugation, the Spanish also brought, for better or for worse, religion. I saw this firsthand at a place called Isla de Flores, Guatemala. One afternoon, the Iglesia Nuestra Señora de los Remedios hosted a celebration. While not religious, I was curious.

I walked through the huge wooden double doors at the rear of the church and moved toward a youngish-looking supplicant.

"Buenos días!" I whispered. "Qué pasa aquí, por favor?" (What's going on here?)

"Esto es la celebración del Jesús Negro," the young Guatemalan woman standing next to an eight-foot-long crucifix of the Christ replied. (This is the Celebration of the Black Jesus.) The crucifix was being displayed supine instead of vertically. I watched as a long line of supplicants waited patiently to kiss the knees of the Black Jesus.

"Estaba un milagro!" she proclaimed. (It was a miracle!)

What miracle? I wondered.

This church overlooking the central square was filled with dark-skinned men, women, and children. The Western-style dress couldn't camouflage the angular features of the faces that looked a lot like the native people portrayed by Diego Rivera in several of his murals on display at the Palacio Nacional de Mexico in Mexico City. Seeing so many devout Maya bowing at this icon of Catholicism was proof of the missionary zeal of sixteenth-century Spain and one of the inescapable consequences of colonization.

If you are a true believer, then you know that miracles can happen anywhere. This one is claimed to have happened in this little town in the northern reaches of El Petén region.

"Por qué está el Jesús negro?" I asked in a hushed voice, inquiring as to why Jesus was black.

An elderly woman holding a votive candle overheard me.

"Some years ago," she began, "a cathedral near here burned to the ground."

"Sí, señora," I whispered. (Yes, ma'am.) "Y después?" (And then?)

"After the fire," she continued, "the church burned to the ground." Her eyes never turned away. "But not the Jesús. It was only charred black." She turned with her votive candle back toward the altar.

When the Roman Catholic Archdiocese of Santiago de Guatemala learned of the miracle, it sent word to transfer the charred crucifix to Guatemala City. While en route, the transport vehicle broke down. The people of Isla de Flores took it as "un otro milagro!" (another miracle!) and interpreted the second miracle as a sign to keep the Black Jesus right here.

I bet the Vatican in Rome didn't know it had a Black Jesus in its genealogy. Regardless, on the Island of Flowers, the Celebration of the Black Jesus is held each January.

Most of the visitors to Isla de Flores and its sister city across the lake, Santa Elena, come here to take advantage of the proximity to one of the great sites of the Maya world, Tikal. It is just an hour or so away by minibus. Tourists fly into the Aeropuerto Internaciónal Santa Elena, spend the night in one of the Western-style hotels, drive off to Tikal the next morning, take the obligatory picture, and then fly out that same day, heading back to the frosty margaritas of Cancún. They have done Maya and they have the photograph as proof.

My experience of the ancient Maya world with our survey team in Belize was clearly quite different. We never had margaritas. We never even had glasses. What we did have, though, were border connections to La Unión, and for us that was our Cancún.

Tourists do, at times, overlook everything. Maya rocks are Maya rocks, as beautiful as they are. When you consider the Maya civilization, though, you have to set down your margarita and pick up a slide rule. Or open up an Excel spreadsheet if you missed that last reference.

The Maya Empire enjoyed a sophistication equaled only, perhaps, by its putative brutality. Over 2,000 ago, Maya astronomers calculated the length of a solar year as $365^1/_5$ days. They predicted solar and lunar eclipses. Ritual temples were constructed with astronomical precision to greet the rising eastern sun.

Maya principles of mathematics and engineering were so advanced that these concepts of calculus are used to this day. It is noteworthy that they based their calculations upon a vigesimal numbering system, a scheme that uses 20 as a base unit. The Maya apparently derived this concept from the sum of ten fingers and ten toes.

For comparison, consider that the Yuki Indians of Northern California count using an octal system, with 8 as its base unit. Unlike the Maya, the Yuki, it seems, count the spaces *in between* their fingers.

European cultures came to use a Hindu-Arabic numbering system about six hundred years ago that has 10 as its base unit. The last time I ordered a pizza from Pizza Hut, I used the decimal system to make change.

There's no right or wrong to any of this. There's vigesimal. There's octal. In either case, pre-Colombian Native Americans knew their way around a mathematical equation. I won't even get started on an abacus.

The point of all of this math history is that in spite of its advanced culture, the Maya civilization vanished about a thousand years ago with no good explanation why. To this day, their extinction just doesn't add up.

Personally, I like the Yuki Indians' awareness that the spaces between their fingers are as important as the things that create the intervals themselves. It reminds me of a discussion I once had with a group of Hawaiian slack-key guitar masters. Some musicians think that making music is the result of fingers and frets. Others assert that music also exists in the silence between the notes.

Fingers plus toes.

Or just the spaces between fingers.

Sound.

Or silence as sound.

A thousand years later, the discussion continues.

The Maya were also adept chemists. They were not so great at filling out forms. Evidence supports the claim that the process of vulcanization, curing tree sap into rubber, was discovered by the Maya twenty-five hundred years before Charles Goodyear filed for a patent.

Holding their society together into a unified realm was a strong central government with a bureaucracy that managed food production, water, trade, and provided for the common defense. These political, artistic, and scientific aspects of the Maya world defined the Maya belief in a heaven as well as a place of fear in the afterlife called Xibalba.

Our survey lives were much more mundane than the intellectual discussions of Maya society. Instead our daily survey existence consisted mostly of early morning truck rides for nearly an hour past Wari Camp and the Río Bravo.

Whether I was driving past Wari Camp or just waking up at the PBAP, I loved the morning. When the sun was still low on the horizon, the light hadn't yet acquired its equatorial intensity. The green in the leaves of the canopy glowed brightly in a hue that was five parts yellow and one part blue. Colonies of army ants flowed across the jungle floor while bees buzzed above. A flock of noisy chachalacas screeched good morning through their sharp beaks. The baritone howler monkeys in the canopy yowled.

This may have been life awaking in the beginning of a new day, but this was life as it has always been here. The fingers of ice of the last great glacial age fifteen thousand years ago never reached down to this latitude. Life here has continued uninterrupted for eons. This was really an old day being relived all over again. It was new only because we were.

Quadrant no. 9 was the focus of our last push before camp ended this summer. I volunteered to lead the survey headed north and teamed up with Esau, our Maya guide, and Cathy, a student from New Mexico. Laura and her group would handle the area east.

We staked out our mutual reference point, from which I shot a northing and Laura shot an easting. I withdrew my machete from its sleeve and began to cut a trail, pulling a tape every twenty-five meters. Cathy charted as we went, hoping to record bearings if any structures appeared.

We moved in twenty-five-meter segments for one-quarter of a mile. Then I pulled a tape twenty-five meters headed due east, and schlepped southward until we were once again parallel with our beginning survey flag. I went left, pulled the tape twenty-five meters due west, and staked another flag. From there I took a northing. And I repeated that same protocol all day.

Simultaneously, Laura and her team headed east at twenty-five-meter sections and, after a quarter of a mile, traversed twenty-five meters north. She and her team would then double back west. She would then head north twenty-five meters and turn east for one-quarter of a mile. Repeat. Repeat. Repeat. This was our survey grid covering an area one-quarter-mile square.

Our effort was, in the kindest word possible, tedious. However, it had an element of exhilaration because of the promise of discovery. For hours we trudged, and measured, and fought off prickly thorns and mosquitoes and tiger ants and beetles, and scanned for vipers hiding below and coral snakes hanging above. It was exhausting, frustrating, dehydrating, hunger-generating, blister-producing, arduous, and wearisome work.

Anthropology-inspired survey attire was functional but less than trendy. The most important gear we wore were knee-high leggings reinforced with copper mesh sufficiently strong to repel viper strikes. These were strapped over boots and long pants.

Walking for miles on a bed of damp, decaying leafy mush required a layer of socks and a pair of water-resistant boots. Ripstop fabric for cargo pants ensured that holes made by punctures would not grow into tears.

Two layers of long-sleeve shirts were sprayed liberally with DEET. Other gear included a neckerchief, a hat, a mosquito net for your face, a machete and sheath, sunglasses, a compass, leather gloves, at least three water bottles, a first aid kit, surveyor's tape, a magic marker, a notebook, a Brunton, and of course, lunch. On more than one occasion, my chosen midday repast consisted of bread and a can of "potted meat food product." Don't ask.

At some point, both teams took a break. Motivated by sheer curiosity, Laura and I scouted an area beyond a rise just north and east of where we were surveying. I cut a trail to the top of a mound. While standing there, I saw the past as clearly as this morning's sunlight.

Stretched below and before me was a Maya plaza. On one side was a collapsed rain structure buried under decayed brush and leaf litter. Immediately across from it was another collapsed building. At that moment I became an accidental archaeologist in a Mesoamerican jungle.

"These don't look like natural geographical occurrences," I shouted in Laura's direction. Confident that these were mounds that the earth could not have arranged with such geometrical precision spontaneously, I asked Laura to come over and take a look.

She plodded over to where I was perched to evaluate the landscape from my vantage point. While she was standing next to me, I suggested cautiously in the presence of Her Professorship, "Maybe these are collapsed Maya structures?"

After some study, Laura confirmed my deduction.

"You're right!" she said with a big smile. "And these structures have never been mapped before. You've made your first discovery!"

Both teams came over to join us and see what all the shouting was about. Satellite villages in the Maya Empire were constructed in relatively the same configuration throughout all of Mesoamerica. That is why collapsed structures covered in dirt and leaves can still be perceived by the relationship of the mounds to one another.

"So what do we call them?" I asked, plotting the GPS points on the map.

Laura thought for a moment and then suggested the perfect name. "We'll call them 'Guy's Group.'"

And there you have it. In the middle of the Programme for Belize Archaeological Project near the Wari Camp escarpment adjacent to the Río Bravo Conservation and Management Area is a Late Classic settlement last seen by Maya eyes between 600 and 800 CE named Guy's Group.

Not settlement #419 or #425, but Guy's Group.

I admit that Guy's Group isn't a Tikal photo op. In fact, if you took a picture while standing on top of just about any mound of dirt in a jungle, it would look like Guy's Group.

You can't see it with your eyes. You have to see it with what is between your eyes. My friend Oscar Berger might not ever experience this joy. Instead, el presidente had flown via Sikorsky over the jungle canopy and, in doing so, had seen everything and nothing.

You can't map the Maya civilization from the air because you can't see the contours of the ground from above. Even when your boots are on the ground, the dense jungle scrub can hide a structure only a few meters away. That is why we surveyed one step at a time, one twenty-five-meter segment at a time, one day at a time. You might see a thousand-year-old collapsed Maya structure if it is right in front of you. But you will never see it unless you find yourself standing in front of it in the first place.

As surveyors, the past was our present. We were required to see Maya plazas, temples, homes, and rain structures where the inexorable forces of time and weather shoved them under leaves, dirt, and fallen trees. Every day we headed out, we mapped what used to be. We were cartographers of the long ago. We searched not for what could be seen but for what our minds knew was there.

Mounds of dirt, leaves, and scrub brush rendered promenades along rain structures and temple plazas nearly unrecognizable, if not impassable. As we tore their earthy disguise away, we brought them to life again. After all of our struggle and in spite of our fatigue, we gazed upon the splendor among the rubble.

Hour after hour, day after day, we hacked trails where human feet hadn't walked in a thousand years or more. We wielded our machetes and took turns from the backbreaking work of cutting through scrub brush and vines. We plodded across muddy *bajo*. We banged constantly on fallen trees before stepping over them to give the snakes on the other side fair warning that a boot was about to fall.

The strong survey. The rest excavate, bitches.

It is self-evident that if you know where something is, it is much easier to find it. That was why Oscar was able to marvel at what fifteen hundred years of neglect had done to the Maya buildings at El Mirador. The buried homes, the rain structures, the temples large and small, were all covered with huge piles of dirt and bush. But el presidente knew what he was looking at.

Unlike the president, we had to imagine the Maya as they roamed the undulating fields of what used to be one of the largest settlements in all of Central America. Stoneworkers. Slaves. Farmers. Potters. Painters. Priests. Jewelry makers. Architects. Bureaucrats. This was life at our ground level.

What I also loved about being here was that it was impossible to resist the authenticity of this experience. In this fabulous Belizean jungle, hundreds of Maya stelae, beautifully, artistically, stylistically carved limestone monuments, stood steadfast and scattered throughout a kingdom that once reached across Mexico, Guatemala, Belize, Honduras, and El Salvador.

To touch any one of these stones was an ineffable thrill. Your hands did not just reach across the distance of an arm's length. Your fingers breached a time bridge of forty-five generations or more. Your hands could caress stones and sense the energy of the man who at one time embodied the power of the present while speaking to the future. All of this existed openly in a faraway jungle.

One epigrapher who deciphered the Maya hieroglyphics concluded that stelae represented banner stones created primarily to glorify the royalty of a particular city or region. In antiquity, a king could erect stone monuments to satisfy his own narcissism and extol the immeasurable majesty of his own achievements.

But the vast geographic openness of the past is now gone. No longer can empires be carved from land like a shirt out of whole cloth. Today, a US presidential library might serve as a banner stone. But clearly, it does not carry with it the same sense of conquest or grandeur.

El presidente could only hope to make his mark in the pages of a history book or, perhaps, in the infinite existence of an e-book on an unseen shelf of an e-library. This was the limiting reality for rulers today. Their desire for immortality was now likely constrained to a generation or perhaps two. They can never be like Siyah K'ak', who reigned supreme in Tikal two thousand years ago and who is remembered, discussed, and studied today as the supreme king known as Fire Is Born.

After weeks of hot days, cold showers, puncture wounds, bug bites, envenom encounters, and potted meat food product for lunch, the time came to strike camp and head back to the world from which we all came. Some of the students and scientists couldn't wait to get back. There were those who could.

For some of the researchers, their lore was built upon adversity. Thus, even if they denied it, they embraced the hardship: a more remote camp, a more rugged site, a more difficult environment. The fewer the niceties at the encampment, the greater the bragging rights. Removed from polite society and campus scrutiny in this faraway jungle, these people became more than they were back home. They sweated more. They talked more. They joked more. But mostly they discovered more. And they brought back more knowledge than they'd had when they arrived.

There were nights of jungle fun. After a few weeks of being in camp, one day a couple students commandeered a pickup truck and made a run into Orange Walk Town for some ice and cerveza. It was Friday night in the PBAP and it was going down.

After dinner and showers, most of the student population gathered in the center of camp to drink iced Belikens, "The Beer of Belize" according to the label, and personal stashes of dark rum, light rum, Jack Daniel's, and some other, questionable beverages.

Grant, one of the camp's lead graduate students, showed up with a canvas lounge chair made of aluminum tubing. Fully constructed, it looked like a La-Z-Boy, complete with headrest, footrest, and beer holder. He jammed a bamboo citronella tiki torch into the ground next to him, lit the wick, and grabbed a beer. We all applauded the audacity of his luxury, jealous that we had not thought of it ourselves.

Night rules at the PBAP were strictly enforced. By 9:00 p.m. we were required to exit camp and hike out to the road a couple hundred meters away to continue drinking and talking and playing music. As custom demanded, we marched out to the middle of the limestone roadway and arranged ourselves in a circle. It was surreal.

This circle in the middle of the jungle in the middle of the summer in the middle of nowhere was comprised of some of the brightest and most self-motivated scholars I have ever been fortunate enough to meet, the likes of whom I may never meet again. Yet there we all sat in the dark, in the middle of a limestone road under the stars, surrounded by a Belize jungle with buzzing cicadas, cold beer, and jungle juice.

Cheerful laughter blended with serious debate. There was music and then silence. Some people drifted off to go to the bathroom.

Some were pointing out constellations. This had to be real, because you couldn't make this up.

The conversations began along scholastic tones: Maya civilization theories, the progress of excavations, the locations of the mapping and survey teams. Then as people begin to relax, voices in the dark revealed how they got here. Some, like me, had come by plane. Others like Grant and Ruth had driven ten days from Texas in a pickup truck.

Then things got silly. Flirtatious comments. Lighthearted double entendres. Good-natured teasing.

"I killed a snake yesterday," a voice from the darkness asserted.

"Really? How big was it?" another voice from the darkness asked.

"Pretty big," was the retort.

"Ah, shit!" was followed by laughter from the voice. "I was in a hole once digging when a three-footer fell into it with me. I killed it with my machete."

Jessie chimed in, saying, "I was excavating a test hole about one foot square," and going on to describe the surface leaf litter, dirt, tree roots, and subterranean bugs. Instead of discovering what she believed were terraced temple stones belonging to an ancient Maya structure, she had found, as she announced to the group, an AFR.

I was taking notes and asked innocently, "What's an AFR?"

She cupped her hands into the shape of a megaphone and shouted for everyone within earshot, "Another fucking rock!"

There was laughter and some applause from the dark. That verified to everyone that I was the new guy.

And so it went all summer. This was their lore. Working. Studying. Sweating. Laughing. Drinking. Teasing. Bantering. Sharing. Teaching. Bragging. Exaggerating. Confessing. Sleeping. Complaining. Helping. Doing. This was the PBAP.

Perhaps these camps were why field anthropologists and archaeologists were such a closely wedded group. The daily work was difficult and tedious enough as it was, but the jungle conditions added heat and dirt and fatigue to an already trying academic effort.

The closeness of camp attendees in their intellectual achievements, as well as in their living and eating quarters, created an atmosphere of tolerance, understanding, and familial-like admiration, loyalty, and respect, perhaps not enjoyed within other scientific disciplines.

People here knew that the person sitting across from them had sacrificed enormously for their effort in Belize. The financial costs were borne by each student personally, which was no small matter. Even if they received course credit, airfare and living expenses could easily exceed $4,000. I can't even envision the nature of the discussions students had when concerned parents inquired, "Is it safe?" I am certain there were a lot of fingers crossed during that talk.

The emotional cost of being separated from loved ones for months at a time can't be diminished.

But every hardship they were forced to bear, they all bore together. That was the connection that separated them from their other associates in academia.

That and the Río Hondo.

SLEEPING WITH THE MOAI

I've slept around.

Take a dart and throw it at a map. Note where it lands. Chances are I've slept there. Or near there.

It's not like I've always slept well. I've been eaten alive in the malaria-mosquito-ridden rivers of Papua New Guinea. I've been brunch for leeches in the Dayak jungles of Borneo. I've awakened in the freezing cold on the flank of Mt. Kilimanjaro in Tanzania before making my way up the Western Breach wall. But as far as memorable one-night stands go, nothing prepared me for sleeping with the moai of Rapa Nui.

It was July 2001. Barely a week before, I had arrived to join a team of anthropologists from the University of Hawaii. I pulled my gear from a pile of luggage that bore luggage tags marked "IPC." Think "Isla de Pascua" (Easter Island), and "IPC" makes sense. Easter Island has been claimed by Chile since the eighteenth century; hence the Spanish translation. In Hawaii, we call it by its given Polynesian name: Rapa Nui.

The journey to Hanga Roa was via a lovely detour. I soared into Papeete, Tahiti, and spent two glorious nights waiting for my LAN Airlines S.A. (aka LATAM Airlines) connection. The flights between Tahiti and Rapa Nui arrived and departed only twice weekly, but as far as I knew, no one complained. Ever.

There is a pervasive luminosity to Tahiti that I have rarely found anywhere else in the world. Women and men parade throughout Papeete with tuberoses or tiare or any other of a number of colorful and fragrant flowers perched behind their ears. In Le Marché de Papeete, vendors, tourists, neighbors, friends, shoppers, lovers, schoolchildren, aunts and uncles, musicians, the hungry, the bored and the tired, mingle in a mélange of joyful laughter with conversations in Tahitian, French, English, Spanish, and the languages of visitors from seemingly everywhere.

"Poission cru, s'il vous plait!" I said, ordering raw fish from one of the fishmongers. The French language made an already delicious dish of raw fish, coconut milk, lemon juice, and vegetables sound even more exquisite. And a breakfast of butter croissants and café au lait brought back sweet long-ago memories of some misspent days in Paris. Intersperse French cuisine of freshly baked baguettes, Brie, pâté, and wines imported from every region of Europe with warm, moist, tranquil days and evenings in the tropics and I discovered that even after I left Papeete, Tahiti never quite let me go.

The gravitational force of these islands may best be illustrated by the tortured yet boundlessly exceptional life of Eugène Henri Paul Gauguin. Tahiti is so enchanting, so captivating, so utterly mesmerizing, that in order to be there, this French postimpressionist artist abandoned his career as a stockbroker; abandoned his Danish wife, Mette Sophie Gad; abandoned his five children with Mette Sophie, as well as several other children from various mistresses; took a thirteen-year-old Tahitian lover, Teha'amana, who later became his wife; died in French Polynesia; and was buried in the Marquesas. If Tahiti can compel a person to forsake marriage, country, and money, then you have been forewarned that your layover may end up lasting longer than you bargained for.

Even though LAN Airlines was an easy flight, there were two landing options at Hanga Roa's Mataveri International Airport. The first was by Boeing 767. The second was by NASA space shuttle. In a questionable act of rationality, Rapa Nui was designated by NASA as an abort site for its spacecraft shot from Florida's Cape Canaveral during the mid-1980s.

The astrophysics behind this decision was simple even if the politics were not. The linear velocity of the earth's surface is greatest at the equator. Thus, Cape Canaveral's 28° north latitude makes it a perfect launch site for space shuttles to slingshot out of the earth's atmosphere using the least amount of fuel possible.

Then NASA developed a plan that ultimately implicated Rapa Nui, though no one knew it at the time. The space agency decided that the Atlantic Ocean was not big enough. It also wanted to shoot shuttles from a desert located near the Pacific Ocean in the US Southwest. That led NASA to ask the air force for permission to use Vandenberg AFB in Lompoc, California, and the Congress for permission to spend about US$4 billion.

An ex post facto inspection of the facilities revealed that Vandenberg had to modify its existing structures to create the West Coast Space Launch Complex, known in cosmos jargon as the SLC-6, pronounced "Slick Six." With a name like that, the whole thing sounds pornographic. In fact, the entire affair ended rather salaciously from a financial point of view as the project was abandoned after all the money was spent.

Even though NASA had billions to spend, not all of the Chileans were queuing up to take some of it.

"The NASA plan is absurd. It's like building a dance floor in a natural history museum!" Chilean historian Oscar de la Barra memorably protested.

Apparently, NASA liked to dance.

What the activists who opposed the plan failed to grasp was the capacity of the United States to ignore Chilean objections. I am fairly certain that no one even asked the Rapa Nui people for their opinion about whether spacecraft and moai would make good roommates on their tiny island.

America's CIA was accused of having backed the coup d'état orchestrated by Augusto Pinochet Ugarte to steal elected power from Salvador Allende. By doing so, the United States now owned a dictator. Throughout Pinochet's thirty-year, iron-fisted regime, the United States' money continued to buy Chilean cooperation. Thus, what NASA wanted, NASA got—like a dance floor in the middle of a natural history museum in the middle of the Pacific Ocean.

Never mind that General Pinochet was accused of assassinating political rivals, murdering, torturing, and disappearing thousands of opposition leaders and their supporters, and otherwise giving new depth to the meaning of the phrase "human rights violations." All of that blood money notwithstanding, that's how the Mataveri International Airport received an estimated US$17 million to extend its runway far enough to land a NASA space shuttle.

As you may have guessed, it was never used. And now with the shuttle program scrapped, it never will be.

Hanga Roa is not just twenty-four hundred miles from the modernity of Santiago, Chile. It is a century away in some respects. For instance, I found a hitching post for horses outside a bar next to a parked car. It wasn't for looks. In a surprising juxtaposition to twenty-first-century spacecraft technology dropping down from the heavens, I saw more than one dark-skinned, long-haired Rapa Nui caballero clopping bareback down the main street on a one-horsepower ride. After seeing that, I was embarrassed to climb into my jeep rental. I realized then how indolence of thought trapped us all. I wished that I had asked the attendants at the rent-a-car stand, "Does anyone know where I can rent a horse?"

Later that week, and by pure chance, I answered my own question. I walked into the Atamu Akena Candy Shop and discovered to my delight that I could buy sweets and rent a horse in the same place. Inexplicably, I didn't rent one. But at least I knew where I could cowboy up if I wanted to.

I walked a little farther until I approached the end of the road. There stood a large, if not out of place, Coca-Cola billboard. The iconic red background displayed the dynamic white ribbon swirling across a row of moai standing shoulder-to-shoulder in place of a series of upright Coca-Cola bottles. Andy Warhol was either laughing hysterically or turning over in his grave.

As odd as all of that sounds, the students attending the University of Hawaii field school were an equally unconventional lot. This group had scholars whose ages were bookended by Thom at fifty-six and Savannah at eighteen. One girl from Wisconsin looked like super-model Christy Brinkley but loved dirt more than lipstick. Michael was an archaeoastronomer. Jacqueline was a curator of a museum in Amsterdam. A dude nicknamed "Corona" from Colorado used the word *cool* in every sentence at least once. And this is only a partial list of the eccentric dramatis personae this summer.

They fit right in on Rapa Nui. Weird. Bizarre. Baffling.

Rapa Nui is known throughout the world for its enigmatic stone monoliths. No one knows what the moai represent, how they were moved, or how they were placed upright. Or the number of people who lived on the island at the time of construction. Or why every single statue that had been erected upright was found toppled when Captain Jacob Roggeveen first made contact in 1722. This was the stone-carving conundrum of Easter Island.

There were all kinds of theories.

There was the one made popular by Jared Diamond, Pulitzer Prize–winning author of *Guns, Germs, and Steel: The Fates of Human Societies*. In his follow-up work, entitled *Collapse: How Societies Choose to Fail or Succeed*, he suggests that the Rapa Nui in their unchecked desire to erect moai decimated their landscape and that the subsequent ecological collapse brought an end to a society that once flourished.

At the other end of the spectrum is best-selling author Erich von Däniken, who wrote *Chariots of the Gods?* He believes that ancient astronauts visited earth and used tractor beams to move and erect the moai.

Recently, two well-respected scientists, Professor Terry Hunt of the University of Oregon, dean of Robert D. Clark Honor College, and Carl Lipo of California State–Long Beach, published their groundbreaking research in *The Statues That Walked: Unraveling the Mystery of Easter Island*. In it they use applied engineering to demonstrate that the Rapa Nui easily "walked" the moai to their locations by rocking them side to side and using their forward center of gravity to generate locomotion.

In contrast to all of this speculation, the hard numbers are enough to make an engineer reach into his pocket protector and break a pencil. Imagine locating a chiseled stone figure weighing as much as a Boeing 747 aircraft. Envision also that this 172-foot, 300,000-pound igneous rock figurine was sculpted without the use of metal tools. Then catalogue 886 other statues scattered across one of the most isolated inhabited islands in the world. That is the beginning and the end of the factual story of Rapa Nui. Pretty much everything else is guesswork.

On the far eastern side of the island stands Rano Raraku Crater, where all of the statues were initially quarried. This makes it the site of the greatest concentration of moai anywhere on the island. From there, the moai were moved to where they were found at the time of Western contact in 1722. But the crater itself remains littered liberally with statues along the slopes of the volcanic cone. Dozens rest in place partially carved, faced upward in a perpetual state of half-creation.

I wandered around for a few days with a lot of people who used -*gist* at the end of the word denoting their job description: anthropologists, archaeologists, geologists, and marine biologists—and other scientists. But all of the -*gist* people bored me. When I came here, I wasn't looking to take measurements, jot down GPS coordinates, review core samples, or sift through dirt with mind-numbing monotony. I wanted something different.

I didn't crave taking a photograph of an immense stone head or dream up some talking points on the mystery of it all. I kept replaying in my head the simple one-word questions of what and how and why, until I scribbled in my journal, "Information is not understanding."

One day while gazing at the magnificent cluster of colossal statues at Ahu Tongariki, I knew I needed to see them in a different way, literally in a different light. So I decided to sleep with the moai.

For me, the nighttime has always been a special phase of the day. The darkness sanctions my mind to unclutter. Once I am freed from blinding sunlight, the shroud of darkness allows me embrace sensations that are otherwise lost in a cloud of visual distraction. The daylight forced me to *see* the moai. The nighttime allowed me to *feel* them. This latter kind of intimacy is reserved for the shadows.

I decided to bed down on the southeastern slope of Rano Raraku Crater after sunset. There were unanticipated issues. The crater was part of the Chilean federal park system. Thus, to spend the night within the boundaries of La Corporacion Nacional Forestal meant engaging in a modest level of clandestine activity.

National parks are closed at dusk. The punishment for a violation of curfew was something about which I could only speculate. So I trekked up the side of the extinct volcano in the dark. As you might imagine, trekking at night can be risky business. I chose to make my way by moonlight after deciding that a headlamp would too easily betray my presence.

The twisting trail took me past a half dozen or so moai buried up to their necks. In spite of the steepness of the crater, I found a small plateau at the foot of one of a group of eleven moai. I placed my head at their feet. As I lay supine, my feet pointed to the stars. I was home for the night.

All over Rapa Nui I remember seeing ceremonial platforms and fallen moai. Disorganized by the careless hands of time, earthquakes, and even tsunami, the ahu were reduced to mere piles of rock. The faces of the toppled moai were buried in the ground, converting their long, smooth backs into huge stone ramps angling heavenward into nothingness.

Looking at these toppled stones was like gazing at a stopped watch. For the Rapa Nui, it was their time coming to an end.

While tucked in my bag, I replayed the comments and cynical laughter of a group of students as they watched the 1994 Hollywood flop *Rapa Nui*. In spite of what the film suggests, no one really knows what the moai signify. It was Hollywoodologists who had written the script for the film, which explains why they thought they had all the answers.

Some of the -*gists* believed that the moai represented chiefs, the spirits of important ancestors, or other powerful members of Rapa Nui's past. There was also the theory that the moai served as a means to communicate with the gods. This explains, according to some -*gists*, why the moai were placed onto ahu. In such an elevated position, they appear to reach from earth into the sky to mediate between here and the heavens above.

Enough. While lying there quietly, I found that after a few hours the scientific noise banging around in my head finally stopped. I watched as the soft shimmer of the moon's glow disappeared into a passing cloud. The change in light brought me back to the warmth of my bag and the beauty of night dreaming.

I was struck by how the face of the moai above me maintained its rigid stoicism as if he had been carved yesterday. His features were vigorous in the silhouette against a nearly black sky interrupted only by tiny points of starlight. Eventually, I closed my eyes and left the moai to stare outward as if awaiting the return of those who had left them here.

Every so often a disturbance made me open my eyes. When I did, I saw a sky that was falling all around me. Stars streaked in every direction of the compass in short bursts and long sparkling arrows. I thought of John Keats, who published his epic poem "Endymion" in 1818. Even though he wasn't describing the night sky over Rapa Nui, he could have been, as he wrote of a place where "shooting stars darted their artillery forth."

The total absence of light pollution rendered the heavens visible all the way to horizon. I easily drew imaginary lines with my finger to connect the glowing dots into familiar patterns. Alpha Centauri and Beta Centauri became the mythical half-man, half-bull centaur. The radiance of Ares, Greek for the planet Mars, was in a rare alignment within inches of his rival, Antares, found in Scorpio. And it wasn't until 4:30 a.m. that familiar Orion would finally throw his shoulders up over the earth's rim.

The sound of crickets mixed with the rustling stalks of dried grass. From within the crater, sea hawks screeched to make their presence known. Down below, an impatient rooster crowed hours before dawn. Cattle called to one another.

I had assumed erroneously that sleeping with the moai would mean a night of silent repose. Instead, everything around me had something to say. Even from a mile away, I heard the Pacific Ocean as it pounded bass notes onto Rapa Nui's steep and dramatic cliffs.

By morning, I watched as this bully of a sea covering more than one-third of the surface of the earth pulverized Rapa Nui. The Antarctic Circumpolar Current rushed along the Chilean coastline unimpeded until it collided into the island's jagged, jet-black volcanic coastline. The crashing waves suggested Rapa Nui was in the earth's way.

It was a wonder in and of itself that early Polynesians had managed to land onto Rapa Nui's shores. Legend has it that the first voyagers arrived here over a thousand years ago and were from the Marquesas led by Hotu Matua. How the settlement of Rapa Nui came about is as perplexing as the mystery of the moai themselves.

Consider that the Pacific Ocean is more than 166 million square kilometers. It is larger than the Atlantic, Indian, and Arctic Oceans combined. In contrast, Rapa Nui's total land area is a measly 177 square kilometers. It is an island, that is 1 million times *smaller* than the body of water within which it is situated. Rapa Nui is a place that should have been lost to the sea forever.

In spite of all of the reasons why neither the moai nor I should have been on the slopes of this extinct volcano, there we were. With the surf pounding in the distance and the winds swirling through Rano Raraku Crater, I slept with the moai.

I awoke under the soothing light of dawn and sat upright to face the same sea the moai have greeted for centuries. At that moment I didn't care what the statues meant. It was enough simply to be there. And as we all stared together toward the infinite horizon and the nothingness of the sea, I wondered, *Why am I here?*

AND PLEASE DON'T LET
HIM GET SHOT

Kirsty used to be a spy.

The Indonesian secret police knew her as "Ruby Blade," a name she chose because she thought it was clever to use "Blade," since her family name was "Sword."

"I does have a nice ring to it," I commented.

Several weeks before in the heat of the summer of 2002, I landed in Dili, East Timor's capital city, with an assignment to write a story I called "The Newest Country of Earth." Even though the war had "officially" ended in 1999, Indonesian sympathizers persisted in committing acts of violence in protest against East Timor's recent freedom from Indonesian rule.

It was my first experience in a war zone. I saw the devastation of the war everywhere. The threat of hostility was also evident as armed United Nations soldiers were deployed throughout the city as well as the countryside as part of the peacekeeping force. The lingering danger wasn't surprising given the fact that Indonesia had waged a brutal war for twenty-three uninterrupted years.

The viciousness of the civil war was such that at its conclusion, almost all of the politicians, intellectuals, businessmen and businesswomen, and health-care providers of East Timorese society had been eliminated. Dead. Disappeared. Gone. Not to mention the tribal and family elders of an entire generation.

Benjamin Franklin once wrote that there was never a good war or a bad peace. The East Timorese in the South Pacific were learning that same lesson two hundred years later. It had been estimated that one-third of the population, nearly 250,000 East Timorese, had been killed in the war. By the time all of the hostilities had ceased, the fledgling democracy was trying to flourish within a population where one-half of the civilians left alive were under the age of twenty. In the presence of having lost everything, still there was hope that there were better days to come.

"I thought Agatha Christie would have approved," said First Lady Kirsty Sword Gusmão with her signature smile. She bounced her young son Kay Olok in her lap while we talked.

I met with the first lady on a Sunday at her home in hills of Balibar, East Timor. I had flagged down Estaves as he drove past my hotel headed in the direction I needed to go. His vehicle wasn't a taxi. There were no such things in a war zone. There were just cars going your way, and others that for the right amount of money would go your way.

"Oh, you mean you want to go to the Lady of Balibar!" Estaves said, correcting my directions.

"Yes!" I said, thinking that sounded close enough.

Soon after Estaves began driving me, he popped a cassette tape into the car's player and sang along enthusiastically: he was "livin' that honky-tonk dream!" This was what a new democracy looked like in this tiny island nation of East Timor. With the help of Alan Jackson, Estaves was singing "Chasin' That Neon Rainbow."

"I go home to Bobonaro when I want," said Estaves, turning toward me and taking his eyes off of the roadway. "No more Indonesian police. No more papers to show."

We arrived high in the mist above what one UN police officer called "Muzzle Beach," which we could see in the distance below. Estaves pulled up to the front of the home occupied by East Timor's president and first lady. I waved goodbye and then turned to do something I have never done before: knock on the front door of the home belonging to the president of a country.

Kirsty came to the door with one of her young sons on her hip.

She was casually dressed, and exuberant that I interrupted her from mommy duty. I followed her to their family's living area, which was modestly furnished with traditional East Timorese textiles, family pictures, a couch, sitting chairs, some end tables, and scattered children's toys.

She was charming and charismatic, so much so in fact that I quickly felt as if we had been school friends catching up since her inauguration as first lady.

"Madam First Lady?" I said sheepishly. "I wish I had a more appropriate gift for you and Mister President, but all I have is this box of macadamia nut chocolates I brought with me from Hawaii." It seemed like a good idea in Honolulu, but now it felt lame.

"Chocolates!" She glowed happily. "We adore chocolates! I'll save them for later." I think that's what she said. I was red-faced with embarrassment by then, and when that happens, I go deaf. This is not an esteemed quality in a journalist by the way. I am supposed to see and hear everything.

"Would you care for something cold to drink?" she asked. "It's dreadfully hot today."

"Thank you," wobbled out of my mouth, as I was still a little nervous, "water would be great!" I really wanted a gin and tonic.

She disappeared.

Servants? No.

The first lady returned after a few moments with young Kay Olok still on her hip. We settled in and I opened my journal.

"So, how did you break into the spy business?" I began with a grin.

"Well, I can say for myself, anyway, that I don't believe anyone grows up thinking one day they will be the target of police intelligence forces," said the university-educated classically trained ballet dancer.

"Something got you there though," I prodded, "aside from falling in love with the rebel commander."

"Yeah. I moved to Jakarta to continue my work with an

Australian aid group," she explained. In the interim, she admitted that she had "read about and knew of Kay Rala and, of course, Indonesia's invasion of the island."

She stood up to rock Kay Olok to keep him quiet. It was unpleasantly balmy and humid that afternoon. She wore jeans, a loose cotton top, and slippers. She was not Jacqueline Bouvier Kennedy, and Balibar was not Camelot. But she was intelligent, articulate, and fearless—and most exceptionally, an idealist.

The first lady admitted that her darkest time was when her future husband was captured and jailed in Jakarta's infamous Cipinang Prison. President Suharto thought that by removing the head of the East Timorese resistance, the body would die. What the Indonesian government did not count on was the love of an Australian woman from Melbourne whose tenacity gave her the strength to choose a future of bullets over ballet.

I am guessing here, but the first lady's ability to pirouette seemed an odd skill set for a spy with a bounty on her head. Not to mention that few spies attend university, let alone matriculate with degrees in Italian and Indonesian and a diploma in education.

"During that time after he was captured, we started writing to one another when he was in prison. When he found out I was in Jakarta and was sympathetic, he started to ask me to do 'jobs' for the cause. I became the link between him and the resistance in East Timor." She stopped dead in her thoughts and declared, "Oh God, this is all so boring!"

"No, not at all," I said, trying to reassure her. "What I am about to ask you," I said apologetically, "will sound boring."

"Let's see, shall we?" she remarked, rising to the challenge.

"Okay, here goes," I said, without further mea culpas. "So, Madam First Lady, would you say that this was one of those great romantic love stories?"

"Well, yeah, I think so," she agreed with a self-conscious smile.

"Anything else on the subject of love in your life?" I asked, giving her an opening to follow up as she wished.

"Yes," she commented quickly. "That and a good bowl of pasta!"

My arrival into East Timor had come with more than one fore-warning. While flying from Singapore to Denpasar, I spoke with Marvin, a flight attendant who was Chinese but who spoke with the most eloquent British English accent. He was surprised when I told him I was not vacationing in Bali but connecting through to East Timor.

"Aren't you afraid?" he asked.

"No," I replied. "From what I have been able to discern, things are better now." Even after I said it, the words didn't sound very convincing.

"My brother," Marvin continued, "was in the Malaysian army as a medic. He was sent to East Timor during the withdrawal of the Indonesian army." Marvin looked serious. "There was a lot of killing there." Pause. "He was happy to come home."

As I waited in Denpasar to depart to Dili, I met Olandina, who echoed Marvin's sentiments. Olandina was a gentle, fif-tyish East Timorese woman. We both waited patiently as the departure announcements teased us with ever changing later departure times.

Headed home, Olandina was my first glimpse into a tragedy ignored for decades by most of the world. She asked me if I knew what I was going to do after I arrived.

"Not quite sure just yet," I confessed. "Find a place to stay, poke around the city, and interview some of the local people about life in their new country. I also want to see if I can arrange an interview with President Gusmão," I expressed optimistically.

"I am afraid when you meet the woman there, many are widows. The war was bad time," Olandina confided. Clearly she was trying to prepare me as politely as she could for what I was likely to discover upon our arrival. Olandina's words were solemn, but she was not what you might describe as sad.

Maybe her sanguinity was due to Mizé, a young girl traveling with her. At four, Mizé had been put in jail in Jakarta with her biological mother and remained there for nine years. At some point in time, Olandina became Mizé's mother.

"Many *maubere*," as she referred to her native countrymen and countrywomen, "tens of thousands of maubere, went into the Indonesian prisons during the war and never came out." Olandina talked about her children and then the others she had taken in: the orphans, the neglected, the abused. The police were known to drop off battered women who had nowhere else to go.

"I have twenty-two peoples now, I think!" she said with joy in her voice.

"And your husband?" I asked, after scribbling a note in my journal.

"I yam, how it sayd, widow?" she said deliberately. "De Indonesian army, day keel heem. My husband. In 1979. But I steel have family."

I appeared outwardly mortified at my insensitivity, but Olandina immediately forgave me. "Esokay!" she said. "You could not know."

We parted at baggage claim. I watched as someone drove up in a truck and she and Mizé pulled away. Olandina had given me her mobile number. I'd said I would call her once I settled in. She worked with the first lady at the Alola Foundation and said she could help me with the arrangements for an interview. I thanked her sincerely and wished her farewell.

She had given me fair warning. I never forgot what she had said throughout my entire stay in East Timor: "The war was bad time." I had no idea then how often I would hear that same refrain. I stopped asking people about their relatives because I already knew the answer.

As we taxied into Comoro International Airport, I peered out through the airplane window trying to gather a first impression of the war zone within which I was going to set up residence for the next month or so. As we approached our gate area for Immigration and Customs, I saw four white trucks all bearing "UN" in block letters on their hoods. There were also three helicopters with "UN" painted on their sides. Later that day at the City Café in central Dili,

I counted no fewer than nine trucks, cars, and vans all bearing the large black letters "UN."

It was reassuring and worrisome at the same time. Perhaps it was all the weaponry. There were rifles and sidearms everywhere I looked. The peacekeeping forces from the Philippines wielded US-made M-16 rifles. The PKF from Australia preferred the Steyer Mannlicher assault rifles. And the PKF from Slovakia were armed with the AK-47s. All of this seemed to suggest that at just about any time, things could suck really fast. That was the first time I realized that there was a very real possibility I could get shot.

I walked up to a waiting car in the car park and asked if the driver could take me into Dili. There was no meter and no word like *taxi* anywhere. I was used to this kind of travel, though. For a price, any car can take you anywhere.

He threw out a price. I threw out a different, lower one. He gave me another. Then I got in.

"I am Guy," I said. "Oh, and I need a hotel. Something clean, safe, and cheap. Do you know one?"

Silence.

Eventually, my driver told me he was Zoni Ximus. That sounded made up to me as I wrote "ZX" in my journal. Or maybe in the custom of certain foreign countries, his name was Ximus Zoni, as one's family name is said first, followed by one's given name. Then he would be "XZ." That explained why so many people I met in my travels called me "Mr. Guy" when I introduced myself as "Guy Sibilla."

Regardless if he was Zoni Ximus or Ximus Zoni, or if the whole thing about his name was simply a fiction, ZX chewed *buah*, a paste made with betel leaf and areca nut that had the awful side effect of staining one's teeth a bloody red color. It was a ghastly look when a buah chewer smiled. Mostly men gnawed it all throughout the Pacific and Southeast Asia. It was a disgusting practice, as sidewalks and walls were often pockmarked with red commas from men spitting out their repulsive red saliva.

As we pulled away from the airport, only then did I realize how grubby the interior of the car was. Grime, grease spots, and patches of foam cushion poked through the seat fabric. The windows were eternally down. Maybe there weren't any. It didn't matter, because the heat was as dreadful as you might imagine tropical heat to be. Moving air was best given the lack of air-conditioning.

From where I sat, my Toyota Corolla appeared to have died quite some time ago, but it was somehow exhumed and made functional. The front passenger's door was painted red, but the rest of the car was white with rust highlights. There was no radio. Given the sound coming from below, there was no muffler either. And were those bullet holes?

I knew then that no one had inspected this car for brakes, lights, horn, seat belts, or emissions, or done any other kind of regulatory safety check, since the invasion of 1975. It did seem a trifling matter considering the ubiquitous presence of automatic weapons, handguns, and armored personnel carriers.

ZX did not speak as we wound through streets that had little traffic aside from UN vehicles. There were no road signs that I could see. Or traffic lights. Or crosswalks. Or people to cross within them.

Now that I think about it, most of what I saw en route was roadside trash and dust devils. There wasn't much of anything except rows of empty, charred, burned-out structures. Being that this was the capital of East Timor, the only word I can think of to describe how I felt at that very moment is a word I have never used in over thirty years of writing: *creepy.*

Eventually, we pulled up in front of the Dili Hotel. From what I had just witnessed driving through town, this seemed to be the only choice. It had no street number, no marquee, and no automatic doors. It was just the Dili Hotel on Avenida Sa da Bandeira.

"Thank you!" I said, as I gave ZX some US dollars and waved goodbye. I turned and walked into my new home. Inside I met two young Filipino women. Mylene and Abia worked the front desk and, as I later learned, served as the housekeepers, the concierge, and the cooks—and performed just about every other service a hotel might provide.

As an aside, one Saturday night a few weeks into my stay, I was invited by them to attend the annual AFET banquet, an event sponsored by the Association of Filipinos in East Timor in celebration of Philippine Independence Day. Because my name is Sibilla, either Mylene or Abia, or both, thought I might have been part Filipino. They later joked that my Italian father and my Japanese mother had made a Filipino baby.

As uplifting as Mylene and Abia may have been, the surroundings of my hotel were not. Unless you've been in a war zone, you can't imagine how difficult and disorienting it is to negotiate through a city in the total absence of street signs, streetlights, street numbers, traffic lights, business signs, doors, sidewalks, windows, and any other kind of landmark. At the risk of sounding obvious, all destruction looks the same, and complete destruction looks completely the same. This was Dili when I arrived.

The next morning I was up early and anxious to get oriented.

"*Selamat pagi*, Mylene!" I said in Bahasa Indonesian, bidding the attendant good morning as I dropped my key at the desk.

"*Magandang umaga!*" she replied in Tagalog. "How are you, Mr. Guy?"

"*Baik, terima kasih!*" I continued in Indonesian, thinking that was their lingua franca given their recent history. (Good, thank you!) Then I went into the deep end of the pool, asking, "Mylene, can you tell me where the presidential palace is?"

I pulled out my letter of introduction as if it were the key to the city.

"I want to interview President Gusmão for my magazine." My letter from Mr. Scott J. Whitney, editor in chief at *Pacific Magazine*, stated the following:

To Whom It May Concern:

Mr. Guy Sibilla is traveling on assignment. ... He will be working on news and feature stories for us in East Timor, Papua New Guinea and the Solomon Islands. ... Please afford Mr. Sibilla all possible professional courtesy and assistance in procuring necessary documents, access and permissions to travel.

Noticeably, Scott had left out, "And please don't let him get shot."

I knew immediately by looking at Mylene that I was on my own. That was okay. Been there. So out the door I went. No address. No map. No ideas. I started walking toward the center of Dili, and then I saw a truck with familiar markings.

"Yo!" I shouted while flashing the peace sign at an armored vehicle bearing the letters "UN" painted on its hood. The white Humvee that was stopped at a corner across the street held four bored-looking soldiers.

"Can you guys point me in the direction of the presidential palace?" I shouted over the diesel engine noise. Wordlessly, the driver stuck his thumb out the window, pointed in the direction somewhere behind them, and then drove off belching black, smelly fumes and leaving me in a cloud of dust. I jammed the peace sign back into the air above my head and kept walking.

I plodded along Avenida Sa da Bandeira, a dusty street strewn with debris and trash. Every so often, when I would meet someone walking nearby, I would smile and say, *"Selamat pagi!"* in my elementary Bahasa.

"Can you please point me in the direction of the presidential palace?" was now my constant refrain to anyone I saw. People kept pointing. I kept walking. At some point I began to wonder if they even understood what I was asking.

As I continued my search, I passed soldiers from Thailand, Pakistan, Japan, China, and Jordan. Land Rover Jeeps, Toyota pickup trucks, and GM-built Deuce and a Halfs (two-and-a-half-ton trucks) all bearing "UN" in block letters on their hoods transported men, women, and supplies to wherever they needed to be. Everyone had rides except me.

I learned a few days later that Bahasa Indonesian was the wrong language to choose of the four possible choices: Tetum, Portuguese, English, and Bahasa Indonesian. For Dili to look like this, you have to fathom the darkness of vengeance and grasp the brutality that the defeated Indonesian army meted out to the victorious East Timorese. President Suharto in Jakarta was so bitter in defeat that as his army withdrew from Dili, they "scorched the ground and salted the earth."

The Indonesian army systematically burned every building, shot anyone, anything, and everything that moved, imploded the radio and TV broadcast towers, destroyed the central electrical power plant and water pumping stations, dynamited every bridge, and essentially reset the East Timorese clock to zero. An island roughly the size of Connecticut literally went dark.

This sounded so appallingly brutal that my initial instinct was to discount the reports as being motivated by more emotion than fact. I was wrong. Such cruelty existed in this world. I was surrounded by its aftermath as proof.

"There were fire trucks," said Gino of Timor Gas, "the kind with the nozzles used to spray water to put out fires."

I nodded my head to acknowledge that I understood.

"The Indonesian army filled them with petrol," he said in a strong Aussie drawl, "and they used them like flamethrowers as they drove up and down the streets in Dili."

"Yes," Emmanuel confirmed a few days later during an interview. "They drove down one side of the street and sprayed fire and burned every home and business to the ground. Then they drove down another until all of Dili was on fire."

If that was not enough evidence, this was confirmed yet again by the Justice Center in Dili. In their independent investigation, they collected multiple statements verifying that the Indonesian army drove trucks up and down the streets of Dili, setting fire up one side and down another. The use of an accelerant was proved as the heat generated by the chemicals melted metal roofs, supports, and road signs.

Those who came out of hiding from the jungle after the conflagration were recorded as describing their capital city as "eerily silent."

Sadly, it wasn't just Dili that suffered the rage of the Indonesian army's defeat. Late one afternoon at the bar at my hotel, I met Mike of Australia's Northern Territory government. He acted as a liaison to help Australian businesses bring their much-needed goods and services to East Timor.

Mike was good-natured and a characteristically blunt Australian expat. He had arrived in East Timor right after much, but not all, of the hostilities had ceased.

"Yay," he drawled, "I remembah when we got caught in a fight between two militias. We were evacked by heli to Liquiçá, where we got shot at over the beach. Those were exciting times," he said with a smirk. "What're you drinkin'? Another Tiger?"

"Yes, thanks," I said. Australians are legendarily welcoming, especially when it comes to alcohol.

"Don't drink Bintang anymore," Mike declared, "not after what I saw the Indonesians do to these people. Tiger's a good one, though!"

"Two Tigers, please," he shouted to the bartendress who was just around the corner.

"You've been here a while," I threw out in order to jump-start our conversation.

"I feel like I've been here for a donkey's age," Mike replied.

However long that was. We talked about small stuff: what I did, what he did, travel, family, the future. Then I turned our banter back to what it was like when he first arrived.

"You can't imagine," he began. "You simply can't imagine what a bloody mess it all was." He related his account of a visit to the eastern end of East Timor as an example of how far-reaching and devastating the destruction was.

"I remember driving into the little town of Lospalos. I'd been there before," he said, looking away. Mike had a way of stopping midsentence as he gathered his thoughts.

"As you came up the road from the beach, you saw that everything had been shot. Everything. All the farm animals were dead and still lay in the fields. And the house pets. The homes were burned to the ground. No one and nothing was left alive." Silence.

After a few moments, he continued. "I'm a pretty tough NT guy"—as if he had to explain—"as we drove toward town, there were these huge old trees along the entranceway. They must have been four hundred or five hundred years old."

I could see them in my head.

"As we approached Lospalos, we saw that the Indonesian army had ring-barked all of the trees," he relayed in a quiet voice. "Can you imagine the meanness and spitefulness of it? The sheer hatred of the act of killing all of those trees? With all the devastation that was everywhere, the army would have had to take about half an hour to ring-bark each tree."

"That sounds terrible," I said, even though it sounded like such a cliché.

For no good reason other than that they could, the Indonesian army had burned Baucau to the ground for good measure. To continue their detestable swath of destruction, they also burned Manatuto to the ground for the simple reason that it was the birthplace of the commander of the rebel forces, Kay Rala Gusmão.

By now, I had been in East Timor for over two weeks. And for the first time, I admitted to myself that I had begun to hate my idea for a story titled "The Newest Country on Earth." In fact, I began to hate being in a place so fresh with war dead and their survivors. The fear of being "disappeared" or raped or jailed or enslaved was still palpable in the air. I was repulsed being so close to the hard evidence of human beings' ability to act inhumanely toward another human being for something as ethereal as a flag or as grotesque as money.

I was suffering a crisis of confidence. It was depressing to wake up and drag myself through the streets each day after having a greater understanding of the brutality that had been meted out here for over two decades. It lingered on the faces of the survivors. What in heaven's name was I going to say that hadn't already been said or written by real war correspondents?

Honestly, for a few days I took myself off of the story and just drank. I did not want to interview another widow who was still in her teens or twenties (or pick a decade). I was sick of gathering personal accounts of indiscriminate killing of civilians, pets, and domesticated animals. I had had it with taking pictures of elderly solitary women looking despondent as they sat in the middle of a burned-out structure.

I had simply had it. Period.

And then something unexpected happened. I had been drifting along Dili's deserted waterfront one afternoon. There ahead of me and out at the water's edge, I saw four young boys doing what boys do: they took on various stages of undress and jumped off of a pier into the pristine blue water below. I heard happiness in the distance and saw what joy looked like as these four friends splashed and laughed, and jumped off the pier over and over again.

I walked out to where they were waving so as to not alarm them. I wanted to make them an offer I knew they couldn't refuse.

"Hi!" I said to the group that had formed together. "Who's in charge here?"

No response.

"Okay!" I continued. "I am prepared to offer whoever is in charge here enough money to buy everyone ice cream and a soda if I can take your picture!"

All four hands shot up in the air as the boys moved closer, each one vying for my attention.

I took out a bunch of bills out of my pocket, counted out enough for each of them, and handed the money to the eldest of the group, with his promise and a handshake to take care of everyone. With that, I shot a picture of the four boys, two of whom were swimming nude and laughing as if this was the best day ever. Every time I showed this picture to someone, I told them the caption should read, "This is what hope looks like." To this day it remains one of my favorite images.

Aid workers recorded other, more tangible signs of hope. There were huge sections of Dili where the structures still remained un-inhabited—roofless shells. In the countryside where foreign aid had yet to trickle, entire towns had no roofs. I learned from various local authorities that in conducting their surveys to report on the rebuilding process, progress was measured if they saw a roof.

"If there was a roof, then there was something going on under it!" one NGO representative commented to me.

I realized then how easy it was to overlook something as important and yet as modest as a roof. As implausible as it sounds, a humble roof meant everything to someone somewhere in East Timor. It was evidence of a home. Or more to the point, it represented that there was a future being built.

Meanwhile, I still didn't have the president's interview in my immediate future. Hell, I couldn't even find the presidential palace. Luckily, my search led me to the United Nations' Police Force (UNPOL) headquarters, one of the two police authorities operating in East Timor. The other was the local agency known as the PNTL: Policia Nacional Timor-Leste.

UNPOL's job was to provide civilian security until the PNTL was adequately trained, equipped, and deployed. If the UNPOL couldn't help me locate the presidential palace, then no one could.

A couple of armed guards at the UNPOL HQ gate gave me the elevator-eyes once-over. I dropped my pack and pulled out my press pass.

"Can you please help me find the presidential palace?" I asked, trying to avoid despair in my voice. One officer turned away, walked inside, and then came to the doorway and signaled for me to come forward.

I thrust both of my hands into the air in mock surrender before proceeding forward.

"Is okay?"

The other officer laughed. I was escorted to Officer Zhonghui, a liaison officer who worked out of UNPOL Personnel. She was a Chinese woman from Guangzhou, Taiwan. She was also young, professional, and attractive.

"*Wei! Ni hao?*" I began, fully impressed with my ability to say "Hello" and "How are you?" in Mandarin.

She wasn't impressed, though.

Officer Zhonghui did not know that I had just spoken about 95 percent of all of the Mandarin I knew. I only recalled those words because one of my cousins had worked in Taiwan and later married a beautiful woman from Taipei. I went for the wedding and learned a few phrases from the maid of honor.

"Mr. Guy," she said in a cool, authoritative tone while focused on my press pass, "you are looking for what place?"

"No, no, no," I submitted respectfully, "it's not a *place* I am searching for," thinking she misheard me. "I am looking for the *palace*, the presidential palace."

Officer Zhonghui looked back at me with military stoicism.

"So you are the UN police force for East Timor?" I commented to break the silence. I made it a point never to miss the opportunity to state the obvious.

"Yes," she said quite matter-of-factly. "We are UNPOL, four hundred and eighty-three officers from thirty countries." She handed me a chart indicating that she was one of forty-one officers from China.

"Lovely!" I said, perhaps a little too flirtatiously for the Chinese officer at the desk next to hers. "Okay. I'm looking for the presidential palace. I've been walking around all day and no one seems to know where it is. Can you help me?" I whined.

"Yes," Officer Zhonghui said, with the politeness yet clarity of tone of one in a position of authority. With that, she pulled out a map. In short order, I had a beginning point, a route, and a destination.

"Thank you for this," I said in all sincerity. "I wish there was some way I could return the favor." I went fishing. "If you ever want to grab a Tiger Beer one night when you get off duty, I am at the Dili Hotel. They have a pretty nice bar." With that said, I grabbed the map, picked up my backpack, smiled, and said the last Mandarin I knew, *"Xieh xieh!"* (Thank you!)

PRESIDENT KAY RALA XANANA GUSMÃO

I knew now that my interview with President Kay Rala Xanana Gusmão was looming in my near future. The presidential palace was in the Caicoli District. I spotted a banner above a doorway. There was an elderly-looking dozing guard just inside. The banner read Palacio das Cinzas, which accurately, if not quixotically, described the "Palace of the Ashes." It was not much as presidential palaces go.

I would have missed it entirely except that my attention was drawn to a few goats, pigs, and milk cows wandering to the left of the entranceway. Large portions of the shiny white marble façade that once adorned the building were gone, leaving exposed the unfinished cement wall base. Black and gray patches of carbon scarred the walls where flames once leapt up through windows. And the roof over the entire second floor was missing. Only the concrete trusses remained.

I tiptoed past the dozing unarmed security guard posted just inside the palace doors. As I skulked by him, my sense of fear of being shot as an intruder diminished somewhat given the apparent level of President Gusmão's security.

I heard some voices down a hallway. After turning around a corner, I abruptly found myself in a small room filled with people who were clearly celebrating something. I stood sweaty, frozen, and dumbfounded.

"Can I help you?" a woman asked pleasantly, after approaching me from across the room. Angela was special attaché to the President's Office.

"I am so sorry to have intruded," I pleaded, self-consciously, wiping the perspiration from my forehead with the sleeve of my shirt. I explained to her that I was in East Timor on assignment and hoped to schedule an appointment with President Gusmão in the following days. "Finding this place took some doing," I said, punctuating my remark with a wide grin.

Angela chuckled and waved for me to follow her. In the next moment, I found myself being introduced to President Kay Rala Xanana Gusmão of East Timor, victorious rebel leader, poet-politician, the country's first democratically elected government official in over five hundred years.

"I am so happy to meet you, Mr. President!" I blurted out awkwardly but sincerely.

With the same randomness of chance that had created the unlikely circumstance that had put me face-to-face with President Oscar Berger of the República de Guatemala in the village of Carmelita on my birthday, I ended up crashing President Kay Rala Xanana Gusmão's birthday party.

An audience with President Gusmão ten years earlier would have been memorably more unpleasant. The clean shirt and slacks he wore now were a far cry from the military fatigues he wore then. During the 1980s and 1990s he had been the most wanted leader of the twenty-three-year-long civil war between Indonesia and his Falintil guerilla fighters. It was common knowledge that President Gusmão was no. 1 on the Indonesian army's kill list. Sometimes it's not so great to be number one.

After seventeen years of guerilla warfare in the jungle, President Gusmão was captured on a tip, convicted, and sentenced to life imprisonment. Being betrayed by a colleague is a biblical tragedy that has been played and replayed throughout the centuries. This time, though, the treachery had the unintended consequence of preventing the rebel leader from becoming just another one of the more than two hundred thousand dead East Timorese.

Being held in Jakarta's infamous Cipinang Prison not only kept President Gusmão alive but also gave him a platform from which to promote his cause to the leaders of the free world. In 1997, Kay Rala Xanana Gusmão was allowed to meet with a recently released South African prisoner who had been jailed for twenty-seven years. Soon after that, the media began referring to him as "the Nelson Mandela of the Pacific."

"I am happy to meet you too," President Gusmão submitted with apparent genuineness, "especially since I have only one more year left to live!" He had a boyish smile.

At the close of the war, government statistics estimated that Timorese men had a life expectancy of only fifty-eight years. That appalling fact ranked Timor-Leste in the bottom 10 percent of all nations tiered in the CIA World Factbook. In the years since the end of the war, Timor-Leste has now inserted itself between India and Pakistan as 165th of the 224 nations catalogued.

Given that he was the leader of the Falintil forces, I was certain there were a lot of people who counted Commander Gusmão's life expectancy in days, not years. Be that as it may, only capricious, unpredictable kismet could have put me face-to-face with President Kay Rala Xanana Gusmão on his fifty-seventh birthday.

"Mr. President," I began my questioning with the basics, "may I confirm the spelling of your full name?" I waited to scribble his reply.

"Yes, of course." And he began, "K-a-y R-a-l-a X-a-n-a-n-a G-u-s-m-ã-o."

Pause.

"But Xanana is a name I gave to myself," he clarified.

He could tell from the look on my face that I was confused.

"You know the band Sha Na Na?" he asked.

"Uh, sure," I mumbled. "I think they were a 1950s revival kind of group. Fun music." I was blathering.

"Yes! Yes! That is why I chose it as part of my name. I liked the sound 'Sha Na Na.'" Another big smile. "And please call me 'Xanana,'" he implored. "Everyone else does!"

"Yes, Mr. President," I said, thinking all the while, *There's no way I can call the president of East Timor "Xanana" with a straight face.* Maybe that was the point. It was about time people smiled again. Just listening to President Gusmão say "Sha Na Na" made me chuckle. It also made me want to vote for him.

President Gusmão's path here had been a difficult one. He once studied, at the insistence of his father, to become a priest. Praying for miracles apparently proved more difficult than fighting for one.

He had also worked as a civil servant for the Portuguese colonial government, which left him with a smoldering resentment for colonial exploitation. He had been a journalist long enough to witness the Portuguese government decolonize his country.

President Gusmão also wrote poetry. But when Indonesia invaded East Timor, he put aside his intellectual life and became a fiery revolutionary.

"We have many problems," President Gusmão admitted, as if I were a cabinet minister. "We are such a poor, poor country." What President Gusmão really wanted to say was that East Timor was ranked among the ten poorest countries in the world. It was nearly dead last in per capita GDP.

Wealth, however, can be a relative concept. The maubere refer to East Timor in their native tongue as *Timor Loro Sa'e*, which means "Island of the Rising Sun." It has tropical shorelines with glassy waters rich with reef fish, and lush vegetation fertile with fruit. It has a verdant mountainous region, which supports a coffee bean industry appreciated by connoisseurs worldwide.

Coffee may wake up the world and love may make the world go round, but petroleum provides the money for everything else. For hard currency, East Timor leased exploration rights to ConocoPhillips to develop the Bayu Udan natural gas and oil reserves in the Timor Gap. The revenues were projected at US$6 billion. And this was the small field.

The apple of the eye of the petroleum and natural gas producers was set on what is known widely as the Sunrise Field. Estimates projected that sales and revenues from this project alone could be ten times those of Bayu Udan.

With the petrochemical industry in its infancy, subsistence farming was mostly what the East Timorese did. Even President Gusmão suggested that his large hands were well suited for the pumpkin farming he dreamed of doing once his young country was finished demanding five more years of his life in political service. Winning the war was hard, but winning the peace proved much more difficult than it looked.

Take, for example, the problem associated with inheriting East Timor's extravagantly bloated bureaucracy. Under Jakarta's rule, government jobs were traded for support. Paychecks bought allegiance. Now free but broke, East Timor was in danger of sinking under its own administrative weight.

These civil servants were dubbed ignominiously as Battalion 702 and came to symbolize the gross excesses in government inefficiency: they arrived at work at "7," did "0" work all day, and departed for home at "2." When thousands of government employees were dismissed as part of a restructuring effort, the resentment poured out of the buildings and filled the streets of Dili with an angry unemployed mob.

President Gusmão was the only person who could quell the anger of this unruly horde. He was the definitive and eloquent voice of the maubere people. In his autobiography, he wrote, "I was born in Manatuto. My mother said it was either on the night of the 20th of June or the early hours of the 21st, 1946, in the scorching heat that ripens the rice."

He was everything the Indonesian army did not want to face in a guerilla leader. President Gusmão was not only the voice of the maubere people but also the soul of the resistance. When he spoke to encourage his followers to fight the invading Indonesians, he became every mother's son. When he took up arms, he became every fighter's brother.

Even from prison, he used words to attack Suharto's illegal

grab of his island. He was handsome. He was charismatic. And he was tenacious. He was the four-hundred-pound jungle beast the entire might of the Indonesian military and its economy could not vanquish.

His own jungle home couldn't kill him. He had survived what was known colloquially as "breakbone fever," a disease the West calls dengue. And malaria. He endured dysentery and starvation.

On trial for treason in Jakarta, he defended himself by admitting, "I am resistance leader commander Kay Rala Xanana Gusmão, leader of the maubere resistance against the cowardly and shameful invasion of 7 December 1975 and the criminal and illegal occupation of East Timor for the last seventeen years."

President Suharto once enjoyed a noninterference policy by the United States, Australia, Japan, and most of the world that courted Indonesia's vast supply of raw materials and cheap labor. He was now coming under increasing pressure—and President Suharto didn't do well under pressure. Eventually he acquiesced to a vote on whether East Timor was to remain with Indonesia or join the community of nations. Freedom won.

In President Gusmão's office, everyone in attendance was neatly if modestly dressed in spite of the dreadful humidity and torrid June heat. I wandered through a room buzzing with quiet conversation, purring with polite laughter, and feeling genuinely joyful. Given the nearly complete devastation of their capital city and the horrific body count at the war's conclusion, it was a tribute to a people's resilience to hear "Happy Birthday to You" being sung cheerily, if not melodiously.

President Gusmão had the heavy eyes of a man who shouldered too many memories of friends and countrymen dying in the struggle for independence. Even though he was the head of state for this tiny nation, he was as approachable as a neighbor cutting grass on Sunday.

We confirmed a time to meet in two days. At his insistence I stayed for cake, and then I left him to the celebration with his countrymen he so richly deserved. I traipsed back to my hotel, making sure to pass the UNPOL HQ just in case I might run into Officer Zhonghui. Arriving home in the dark, I showered, changed, and headed out to the bar for some food and a Tiger. With my interview set, I turned my thoughts to the Fijian Peacekeeping Force deployed here.

Editors seemed to know stuff no one else knew. I suspected they were a tight-knit club and regularly called each other. Somehow Scott knew that Fiji had a significant deployment of men in East Timor and he wanted me to write a story.

"Find an angle," he said at our meeting before I departed. "I know you'll come up with something." With that kind of encouragement, I hoped to find if, and how, the Fijian PKF may have brought a special sensitivity to helping their island neighbors.

With that idea and my letter in hand, the following day I set off to find the Fijian military contingent. I kept giving fate a chance as I walked back to UNPOL HQ, this time with a different request. At the gate, I asked if I might see Officer Zhonghui.

"*Wei! Ni hao?*" I said, grinning as I entered her office.

She seemed to smile and frown at the same time, if that was possible.

"I am so sorry to bother you again, Officer Zhonghui, but I am now trying to locate the Fijian PKF. Is it possible for you to help me with that too?"

Culturally, in matters of attraction, it is difficult to tell when you may be treading on thin ice and when you are making forward progress. I was in that spot.

Then Officer Zhonghui smiled and said, "Nice to see you. Yes, I can help." She did. I renewed my Tiger offer before departing.

Soon enough, with Officer Zhonghui's directions, I located the Fijian PKF headquarters in Dili. Their garrison was guarded by a delegation of military police from the Philippines. At this rate I might just meet all 483 UNPOL officers in person. I was amazed to discover that the array of police officers deployed to East Timor came from Bangladesh, Bosnia, Chile, Jordan, Nepal, Niger, Norway, Portugal, Samoa, Slovenia, Sri Lanka, Ukraine, and Zimbabwe, to name a short list. I foresaw some complications.

Here's a cheat sheet. If a Jordanian MP says, "*Shu ismak?*" you should consider telling him your name. If a Nepalese MP points at you and shouts, "*Virāmna!*" then you should stop! If a Ukrainian MP hollers, "*Zamerzaty!*" then you should freeze!

I'm kidding. They all spoke English.

My passport, my letter of introduction, and lots and lots of pleading and begging finally moved one of the MPs to get someone from the Fijian command to come down and meet me at "the Gate." There, I met Major Saladuadua, aide-de-camp to Major Ragogo, commander of the 205-man contingent of the Republic of Fiji Military Force (RFMF) deployed in East Timor. Shortly thereafter, as you may have already guessed, I had a major meeting with Majors Ragogo and Saladuadua.

Maybe it was my island-neighbor trump card as a Hawaii resident. Maybe they pitied the fact I had been sent to the end of the earth. Regardless, after sharing my letter of introduction and discussing how interesting it would be to tell a story of how soldiers from one island in the Pacific Ocean were protecting people on another island, I received an invitation to ride with them the following morning to their advance base on the western frontier.

Major Saladuadua explained that we would head out to the jungle outpost defended by Foxtrot Company. They called it Viseisei, a sacred place in Fijian legend. I wrote "Fort Fiji tomorrow" in my journal. It was the front line against infiltration by militia forces sympathetic to Indonesian rule.

For men constantly regaled in weaponry, the UN forces everywhere in East Timor appeared remarkably relaxed. I found this sense of ease to be incongruous with the ubiquitous presence of gun muzzles and bullets.

In Dili, UN troops lounged calmly in spite of being draped in the gravitas of gunnery. I seemed to be the only one who gave a damn about everyone sitting around bearing holstered .45-caliber sidearms and slung F88 Steyrs—not the civilians ambling along the dusty roads, not the farmers in the markets, not the kids dawdling while at play.

Even if the smiling soldiers sported UN fashion-forward baby-blue baseball caps, it was still disconcerting for me to see all of those shiny gun barrels. Accessorizing with firearms and a tactical vest would be an unusual addition to my wardrobe.

However, one of the great pleasures of waking in East Timor was the coffee. Only two things thrive in the high, foggy dampness of the central jungles of East Timor: maubere villagers and coffee trees. This tiny island bounded by the Banda Sea to the north and the Timor Sea to the south produces some of the best coffee beans in the world. Ask any coffee expert. According to some bean counters, there are nearly two billion of us coffee experts out there.

Like a lot of people, my morning routine tended to be the same even if I was waking at the edge of the Indonesian archipelago. I needed two things to start my day: a hot cup of coffee and a newspaper. On one of my first mornings in Dili, I gave a barefoot little boy a dollar for a paper. Then I flipped the paper open as I sat at a roadside café. I use the term *café* loosely.

Nothing is as enchanting as a surprise, even early in the morning. The first page of the newspaper was written entirely in Portuguese, a language first brought to the island in the early 1600s and one of which I had no working knowledge. The second page was written entirely in Bahasa Indonesian, the language of the occupying force since 1975 and equally unintelligible to me. The third page was written entirely in Tetum. Enough said. Finally and thankfully, the last page was written in English.

Oddly, though, the layout and the pictures were not the same on any given page. From that fact, I deduced that these were not the same pages translated into four different languages but four distinct pages carrying four unrelated news reports.

The very fact that there was a newspaper was a minor miracle.

Perhaps I might have even gone so far as to say my glass was half full. But then again, three pages of my paper were no better to me than fish wrap, so maybe my glass was really three-quarters empty. You do the math.

Regardless of what this seemingly insignificant ritual meant to each of us individually, in East Timor collectively, it meant the war was over. It also suggested that even in horrible places where dark, dreadful, unspeakable things took place, it was the return of the small things that signaled both an end and a beginning.

That's what that morning cup of coffee and a newspaper represented. Nothing so small yet so forceful creates a perception of peace, security, and normalcy. In such circumstances, when you say, "Have a nice day!" as you depart, there is a belief that chances are the day will, in fact, be nice.

I strolled back over to the military base that housed the Fijian contingent on the morning of my departure to their forward base. I was escorted from the Gate to the staging area, where three Land Rovers with drivers waited. I greeted Major Ragogo. Neatly dressed in pressed olive-drab fatigues, he now bore a sidearm, unlike the first time we met in his office. We exchanged hellos. He quickly ducked into the backseat of the center Rover.

At fifty-two years of age, Major Ragogo was one of the oldest and the most respected officers of the Fijian detachment. He had served abroad in peacekeeping missions at Charlie Swing Gate at the Lebanese-Israeli border, Checkpoint Alpha at the Egyptian-Israeli border, Camp Spartan at the Iraqi-Kuwaiti border, and the Paguna mines on Bougainville Island. Now, he and his soldiers were in East Timor. Other members of the RFMF served in the troubled African states of Zimbabwe, Somalia, and Uganda, just to name a few. The Fijians got around.

Major Saladuadua came to gather me from the rear Land Rover and invited me to ride with him and Major Ragogo.

"Thank you, sir!" I said with sincere gratitude. I knew that for military men, this was akin to being invited into the Officers' Club.

The military play by a different set of rules; civilians don't always get chain-of-command protocols. To outsiders, such blind obedience can even seem bizarre. As a civilian, I, by being invited to sit with them, was being given rare proximity. Even though I understood I was pushing my luck a little, after I settled in I asked Major Saladuadua, "May I take pictures as we drive?"

Major Saladuadua looked across at Major Ragogo. With the subtlety of the flap of a hummingbird's wing, permission was granted to Major Saladuadua, who then granted it to me. Chain of command. I saluted in my head.

Major Saladuadua was a soldier's soldier. No matter how hot or dusty or humid it was, he was always as crisp as a Lay's potato chip. He had skin the color of East Timorese coffee, and at 6'5" and 225-plus pounds, he towered over the Filipino MPs. In fact, Major Saladuadua loomed over most everyone on the island. His size so dwarfed his M-16 carbine that it looked like a toy.

After a few soldiers jumped into our escort vehicles, we sped off to Viseisei at Aidabeleten on the northwest coast of East Timor. The road hugged the pristine shoreline as we made our way through several villages pinched between the sea and the lush tropical vegetation. We passed fishermen in boats laden with spiny lobster, octopus, snapper, ulua, tuna, and more.

There were no tourists.

While riding with Major Saladuadua, I learned quickly that he was as gentle as he was colossal. Military regulations required all soldiers in theater to carry firearms at all times. Major Saladuadua was mindful of the fear a weapon could instill in a population so recently terrorized by war. As a result, whenever we left the vehicle, he always draped his M-16 carbine in dark green camouflage netting to make it less obvious to any of the men, women, and children who may be close by.

Several hours later, we arrived at Foxtrot Company HQ at Aidabeleten. As we pulled past the guard tower at Fort Fiji and entered the facility, I was alarmed to see the extent of the fortification.

An Australian PKF had originally deployed here. They had built a fortress that spoke to an imminently larger threat than I had ever begun to contemplate.

When Major Ragogo exited the Land Rover, the camp jumped to life. We walked directly into the VIP briefing room and met a waiting Captain Logavatu, the base information officer. With a look to Major Ragogo and then a nod by Major Saladuadua, the captain began briefing me on the logistical problems of keeping the western border secure from incursions by the pro-Indonesian militia.

Most of the villages in the highlands were so remote that they were accessible only by foot. Consequently, patrols headed out from Fort Fiji for three to six days at a time.

"The bottom line for our guys," offered Captain Logavatu with enthusiasm, "is that if you are not sure how to act, act as if you were back in your village. Go to the chiefs, show respect for the elders, treat the families like you would treat your own." Major Ragogo's troops knew they were a protective shield and not the tip of a spear. There was my story. I shot some photos, interviewed a few of the rank and file, and ate a late lunch at the mess hall.

All too soon I was ordered to assemble at the Land Rovers in five. Very little asking goes on when you are in the service. We returned to Dili later that same afternoon, as Major Saladuadua thought that having a civilian in a forward military base was too risky in spite of their firepower. No argument from me.

When we got back to town, I set up a meeting with Captain Taito at UN PKF HQ. Captain Taito was going to provide me with some statistical data on the UNMISET, the United Nations Mission in Support of East Timor. I talked with him about how the Fijian PKF seemed to fit in well with the East Timorese villagers given their shared island heritage.

"One salt water," Captain Taito said softly. The Fiji insignia on his right shoulder faced squarely toward me as he rotated his chair and turned his jet-black eyes momentarily toward the ceiling. Captain Taito finished his thought sounding more like an anthropologist than a soldier: "We use that expression to convey to the local people in the villages that we are all from the same source. That we are all from the Pacific." This was peacekeeping Fijian style.

With Captain Taito's comment still echoing in the room, I pulled out my journal and reviewed my notes of some comments shared by Captain Logavatu at my briefing at Fort Fiji. I shared with Captain Taito that Captain Logavatu had related that five of the initial RFMF contingent deployed had come from the island of Vanua Levu. While patrolling the remote highlands, a few villagers overheard the Fijians talking. One of the villagers approached the RFMF squad and said it was nice that they could speak Tetum. The Fijians explained that they were merely conversing in their own dialect spoken on Vanua Levu. They said they were never taught Tetum. When RFMF command received word of this unusual event, the five soldiers were reassigned to serve as translators.

Captain Taito was not surprised. "East Timor and Fiji may be separated by one thousand miles of ocean," he opined, "but it is still one salt water." I loved that idea so much, I wrote a story entitled "One Saltwater."

I asked Captain Taito to express my heartfelt gratitude to Majors Ragogo and Saladuadua for all of their special efforts in illustrating how Fiji exemplifies the very best of the United Nations' mission here and around the world.

I returned to my simple but clean room at the Dili Hotel. I took a shower and then had a nap. Life was good.

I awoke hungry. As I dropped my key at the front desk, Mylene handed me a note. It was from the first lady, inviting me out to her home the following day, Sunday, for a chat. Possibly I had made a good impression on the president.

I stuffed the note into my bag and went looking for some food. I ended up on a nearby beach, where I bought a fish from some fishermen who had built a fire. For about US$3, I sat on the edge of their boat and ate my deliciously cooked fresh fish with salt, pepper, and lemon under a dusky pink sky. The old man of the sea gave me a Coke. *Life can't get much better than this,* I thought.

Well, maybe if I had brought some wine it could have been better. I agreed with W. C. Fields. "I cook with wine," he jibed, "Sometimes I even add it to the food." I hear you.

The following day was when I met Estaves, who serenaded me with his rendition of "Chasin' That Neon Rainbow" most of the way to Balibar. After our interview and a few photos, the first lady invited me to accompany her the following day. She had a series of events beginning at the Alola Foundation in Dili and then moving off into the countryside.

The following morning, bright and early, we met at the Alola Foundation's center in Dili. The first lady's Foundation was established initially in response to the sexual violence directed against women and children as part of the campaign against the movement for East Timor's independence from Indonesian rule. Since the cessation of hostilities, the first lady has continued her tireless efforts to improve the lives of women and children there.

Today, she traveled by SUV, with her staff and armed security at a distance. The recent history of the island made the first lady, like Major Saladuadua, hypersensitive to the presence of weaponry. The first lady had never minced words, declaring, "During the war women were raped and widows were made on an shocking scale." Words like these still inflamed the passions of those who sympathized with Indonesian rule. Because of that, the first lady was required to travel with protection.

As she moved through Matata (attending a reconciliation meeting for war crimes), Mirtutu (visiting a primary school in support of education and the women's shelter in support of abused women), and Ermera (visiting a primary school in support of education), at some distance were the calm and watchful eyes of her Australian countrymen, the Assault Pioneers of the First Battalion Royal Australian Regiment. I personally loved that these serious-looking, camo-dressed, Steyer Mannlicher assault-rifle-bearing bad-ass dudes had as their regimental song "Waltzing Matilda."

What East Timor means for the rest of the world is that no matter how dreadful human beings can be, there is always the presence of hope. Sometimes it reveals itself in something as modest as a roof. Perhaps it is the presence of thirty nations who sent their citizens to help another country that many of them may not have known existed until their deployment. And maybe, just maybe, it is one more step toward an understanding that for all of our differences, we're all the same.

EPILOGUE

Even though it has taken me nearly three years to complete and publish this manuscript, I am already looking forward to revisiting this collection of stories years from now. I know that a lot of writers avoid reading their own completed work because the process of writing can be long, arduous, and at times frustrating. But I find reading my past articles and other work helpful in taking stock of own personal growth.

As a traveler, I suspect I will view the events included here differently through the prism of my life as it has developed. The circumstances, the locations, the people, and other details will be the same. But in another decade or so, I will have traveled to other destinations and met other people and shared other experiences. Undoubtedly, these experiences will affect my understanding, my interpretation, and my appreciation of the disparate episodes that comprise my past and make me the person I am.

For that reason, movement is and remains an essential component of how I live my life. What I think something means now might be quite different ten years from now, as each new layer of experience and my memory of those experiences forces me to reevaluate my past and present awareness. Even now, I periodically look back with wonder at the way travel has affected me. I predict my perspective will keep changing as the world keeps shifting beneath my feet.

I am not the only one to believe in the transformative power of travel. One of the most influential writers in my library is W. Somerset Maugham, who suggested the following in his travelogue

The Gentleman in the Parlour: A Record of a Journey from Rangoon to Haiphong:

> I travel because I like to move from place to place,
> I enjoy the sense of freedom it gives me, it pleases
> me to be rid of ties, responsibilities, duties; I like
> the unknown; I meet odd people who amuse me
> for a moment and sometimes suggest a theme for
> a composition; I am often tired of myself, and have
> a notion that by travel I can add to my personality
> and so change me a little. I do not bring back from
> a journey quite the same self that I took.

Like Somerset, I am certain that in years hence I will marvel at my good fortune through the eyes of the evolving person I am constantly becoming.

As part of the process of travel, I engage in meticulous scrutiny and note taking. My journals are painstakingly filled with one-word memory triggers noting the tastes, temperature, fragrances, shapes, colors, sounds, and every other physical sensation of movement. There are also my impressions, like confusion, fear, amazement, illness, delight, loneliness, happiness, and every other notion that arises when an array of details swirls past me faster than I can begin to grasp. I jam receipts in between pages regularly. My journals are part notepad and part scrapbook.

Recording these phenomena allows me to consider and then assess the impact of a journey later in time and within the safety of my home. These notations, together with my drawings, receipts, passports stamps, and the like, is how I get to focus on what happened in the quiet, which allows me to make some kind of sense of it.

That brings me to this final thought. For me, travel has been a lifelong love affair with the world. And like all true loves, it has proven to be unpredictable, and at times astonishing, but always an immeasurable delight. I shouldn't be surprised. After all, the word *joy* is found within the word *journey.*

ABOUT THE AUTHOR

Guy A. Sibilla is a writer living in Honolulu, Hawaii.

In spite of his reckless disregard for his own personal safety, he has managed to travel extensively for over thirty years throughout the Americas, Europe, Africa, Asia, Australia, and the Pacific Basin. His stories and images have appeared in domestic and foreign newspapers and magazines.

As a contributing editor for *Honolulu Magazine,* he received a Finalist award from the Hawaii Chapter of the Society of Professional Journalists for his story and images in *Sleeping with the Moai* (2001).

His life continues to be a work in progress, as is his book *One Hundred Love Sonnets.*